THE
BRITISH ABROAD

THE
BRITISH ABROAD

A Survival Guide

Laurie Graham

Chatto & Windus
LONDON

Published in 1991 by
Chatto & Windus Ltd
20 Vauxhall Bridge Road
London SW1V 2SA

A CIP catalogue record for this book is available from
the British Library

ISBN 0 7011 3656 1

Photoset by Rowland Phototypesetting Ltd
Bury St Edmunds, Suffolk
Printed in Great Britain by
Mackays of Chatham plc, Chatham, Kent

CONTENTS

INTRODUCTION

This book developed from the frustrations and fascination of living in the heart of a British tourist attraction – the city of Cambridge. The seasons of my year were marked by the languages that floated up through my bedroom window late at night. 'Ah! The Italians! Must be July.' The Americans came. But not at the same time as the Japanese. The French came and we couldn't hear ourselves think. The Germans landed and we hardly noticed.

Without them all the city would have developed quite differently. If it had remained a standard item on the English daytrip circuit, we would have a couple of tea rooms, a National Trust gift shop and not a lot else. Certainly not restaurants that are still buzzing at midnight, and probably no pavement cafés. And Sundays we'd be closed, in spite of all those undergraduates bent on pleasure. These foreigners have influenced my city. They make it overcrowded. At certain times of year unworkable. We complain about their demands, their elegance, and the way they ride our bikes, but perennially they make our city a much richer place to be.

The interest of observing them made me more self-aware

when I travelled abroad. If the Spanish and the Swedes and the Malays could all manage enough of my language to ask the way to King's College Chapel, how come I started to sweat as soon as we sighted Boulogne? If I could spot an Italian woman at one hundred yards as she walked along an English street, was the reverse true when I was in Italy? What do our partners in business and in politics say behind our backs? And is it thinkable that the Spanish, most honourable of people, do no more than grit their teeth and pocket our money?

I thought I had a pretty good idea. I believed the British were still a major international presence. Loved and loathed. Admired as symbols of fair play, feared for their bulldog grip, envied for their antiquity, and abhorred for their pugnacious young men. In brief, I thought we mattered enough to arouse strong feelings.

My search for the truth took me round the world. I observed British businessmen doing long stints in the Arabian Gulf, and lightning trips to Japan. I asked the Americans, who allegedly love us, to level with me. And I went to Europe – what am I saying! We *are* Europe! – I mean I went across the water to Greater Europe, to watch, and to ask the natives if they saw what I saw. I visited our Eurocrats in Strasbourg, our sightseers in Venice, our intending commuters in Picardy, and our principal exports to Spain – the polite and elderly who winter there, and those ambassadors of lagerdom, bad and ugly youth.

I learned fast not to ask the natives. To a man they were far too polite to tell me. Early on I was forced back into my favourite occupation – Travelling Eavesdropper. That is how most of the book happened.

My journeys developed like circles on the surface of still water. I began with a day in Boulogne and ended up in Japan. But those readers who would just like the low-down on Frankfurt, or how to behave in Abu Dhabi, or who would simply like to know which gestures are safest left at home, the relevant chapters are clearly sign-posted and can be reached without a detour through Paris or New York. I have tried, anyway, to balance bad news with good advice.

THE BRITISH

Who Do They Think They Are?

When I began writing this book I regularly got embroiled in the following exchange. 'I hear you're writing about the English abroad.' 'The *British* abroad, actually.' 'Same thing.'

It seemed unnecessarily school marm-ish to point out the difference between England, and that amalgam of the Kingdoms of England and Scotland, the Principality of Wales, and Northern Ireland that the world abbreviates as the United Kingdom. In writing of the *British*, I've included them all. Anyone who travels and who considers himself British by birth, accident or habit should count himself in. I've resisted suggestions that I use this opportunity to sort out the grain from the chaff and reveal whether the Welsh travel better than the Scots. When we're far from home, only nostalgic North Americans are remotely interested in that kind of fine tuning, and remotely interested is all they are.

Here, briefly, is our British pedigree. Until 2500 years ago not much to report apart from the odd Bronze Age invasion. Then the Celts arrived. Some of them stayed, and a lot of them headed for the Spanish sun, so nothing new there. The Romans came, saw, conquered, and went. We'd hardly had time to

change the sheets after the Romans had gone, when the Angles and the Jutes dropped by, and the Saxons settled in for a century of serious territorial grabbing and settling.

Some of the Irish Celts who hadn't gone looking for a sun-tan then invaded Scotland and got windburn instead. And further south, the Angles and Jutes sent postcards to Denmark saying 'Rich pickings. Wish you were here?' and the Vikings took the hint. In fact they got their feet under the table for a couple of hundred years. Then those Normans landed.

For the last 924 years things have been pretty quiet. Jews were welcomed. Jews were expelled. Then they were welcomed again. Some people arrived and remained separate, some were assimilated fast. Huguenots, Gypsies, Russians, Poles, Indians, Pakistanis, Bangladeshis, West Indians, Africans, Cypriots, Chinese, Vietnamese. For me, this amazing gene pool makes it rather petty to enquire 'And what is the position of your book *vis à vis* the Welsh?'

My position on the Welsh is that whilst they are not English, nor even a deviant strain of English, they are certainly British. I understand how their proud regionalism has been inflamed by the presence of English house buyers who've really had it with

Fulham and want to keep goats, but it is irrelevant to the themes of this book – first impressions, stereotypes, and reputations that stick like mud.

I have done my level best to spread the dirt evenly. If there's any regional sub-section of the British travelling public I've overlooked or failed to insult, I can only apologise.

STYLE

What *Do* We Think We Look Like?

I noticed many years ago that wherever I was in the world I could recognise a Brit. Sometimes an instinctive suspicion was confirmed by process of elimination – North American, perhaps? No, in North America those teeth would never have escaped the predations of an orthodontist. Belgian? No. Too much reckless use of colour and pattern. I didn't like the way the British looked, but I did find something comforting about being able to spot them on the far side of the Place de la Concorde.

The more I've travelled, the gladder I've become about our wilful disregard of the fashion scene. It suggests an admirable national self-confidence, a people too engrossed in issues of importance to have time to worry whether the gloves and bag should match. The truth is slightly different.

We are hampered two ways on our road to elegance. First, we have a very poor sense of how things look. It dogs us in the carpet department, and trips us up when we create a salad. It allows us to make window displays out of packets of corn plasters. Fair enough. We can't be good at everything. But there's something else. We're not really sure that *elegant* is a *nice* thing to be. The British are much more comfortable with a threadbare old faithful or something cheap. 'It'll do' could be our national motto.

I should nail my own colours to the mast. I do not own a classic cashmere cardigan, or an eclectic collection of fine silk scarves, and I've never had a manicure in my life. But the basis of that co-ordinated knock-'em-dead *chic* at which even foreign schoolchildren succeed and rich Brits spectacularly fail has always interested me.

We seem to be the world's greatest wearers of floral frocks and nylon T-shirts. We have cornered the market in white cardigans. Taken the black city shoe to places where others wear flip-flops. And found more clever ways to wear a quilted body warmer outside a stable yard than its creator ever dreamed possible. What's more, beneath the sartorial jumble we are unkempt and slovenly. We spend money on a new greenhouse when we could be getting that cellulite zapped.

There is something reassuringly *steady* about a nation that eschews plastic surgery and nail sculpture. I'm told by beauty therapists that there are whole areas of potential self-improvement that British women ignore. We're soap and water people, wary of creams. We scrub our faces and neglect the rest. We approach all lily-gilding with a kind of embarrassed impatience – a *dab* of powder, a *dab* of scent – the British are great dabbers.

Certain parts of the body, over which other people refuse to admit defeat – the bosom, the thighs, and the gnarled and weary foot – we never tamper with. We strip off when the sun comes out and whether or not local custom allows it, but not in a state of oiled and pummelled splendour. And we hang on to those gardener's hands. To the British, three layers of nail polish seems like vanity at its most dissolute.

9

But what do we actually look like? Lumpy and discordant. Hectic. Ungroomed. Random collisions between our bodies and our wardrobes, and on special occasions our charge cards. We still have a strongly developed sense of dressing up and having everything match. Lack of fit or loose buttons don't interest us when we've just spent £100 on a yellow peplum jacket and we have only three weeks left to accessorise. Mainly we seem like we never look in a full-length mirror.

There is a type of British woman who is generously cut in the beam. She is the principal wearer of the dropped waistline, a style it's very difficult to avoid in British dress shops and which effects the optical illusion that a woman with a merely large bottom has had it inflated with a foot pump. Only one thing can make matters worse – the bunched, elasticated hemline of a pastel anorak – and usually it does. This is a Basic British Look. But there are others.

We are drawn inexorably to some of the least flattering colours in the world. Approach any group of British women over the age of 60 and you will find that at least seven of them are wearing off-green raincoats. Choose a younger group, in their 40s, and there will be a significant showing of white tights.

Focus on the young and you will find a whole nation within a nation that wears a short, tight denim skirt and white stilettoes with legs that would look handsome on a butcher's slab.

We love track suits. We love them so much we wear them with court shoes and a handbag. We love shoes with clever little details like a spotted bow at the back, so we wear them with chinos. And because of our native climate, we never neglect to take a perfectly nice outfit and ruin it with a woolly.

In New York, where women combine tailored wool with running shoes and it isn't hard to be well-dressed, I tried to find a Brit who would scupper my unpatriotic theories. On Wall Street I couldn't find any men in brown suits and Brylcreem. On the Upper East Side I couldn't track down any green macs or white legs. The place was full of Americans. But in Greenwich Village, between West 3rd and Bleeker, I came face to face with my heritage.

She had patent heels, sheer black stockings, a kilt in Dress Stewart, a duffel coat, sheepskin mittens, and an umbrella with a teddy bear handle. He had the bottom half of a suit, trainers and an Aran jumper. They were from Hatfield. They were very nice. And only the worst details of their appearance have been withheld, to protect those of a sensitive disposition.

What are we? We are courageous. We are largely unshackled by fashion. And at any given moment we like to feel that we are perfectly dressed for making jam or meeting the Queen. Proportion doesn't interest us, and neither does finish. We have that uneasy kind of relationship with hairdressers that exists between man and pit bull. And we see no reason at all not to plump for apricot polyester just as long as it doesn't need dry cleaning. If that isn't style, I don't know what is.

11

FRANCE

Similar, But Worse

The British in France

Having neighbours is often a strain. Even when they don't invade you for hundreds of years, there they are, evolving, differing, *existing*, and some of them less than 30 miles away. According to popular French mythology, the British were a chilly class-riven nation of ascetics, masochists, and snobs. According to the Brits the French were libertines. Not surprisingly, the British have always been much more willing than the French to cross the water and test their views.

The drift of Brits to the south and south-west of France has been a middle-class phenomenon, a search by earnest and enthusiastic francophiles to buy a place in the sun and live like locals. It is a manifestation of the British yearning to get back to the land, mix with *real* people, and it has the exotic attraction of being foreign. On the eve of 1992 this scores high on the charisma scale.

The lop-sided love affair between the French and British amounts to this – they get more sunshine than we do, and it is still possible to buy a five-bedroom heap of rubble for under £30,000. As for lifestyle, sense of nation, sense of self, the differences are small but significant. Far from being insufferably foreign to one another, we are uncomfortably alike. Like sisters who've been through different schools, each of us is proud of the evident superiority of our *alma mater*, but holds the other in affectionate regard.

We look different. To the great anguish of British women who like the idea of elegance but are bonded to old cardigans, the French are deliberately polished. On one side of the Channel there is a humourless pursuit of cut, line, and colour, an unwillingness to compromise with nasty buttons or frowsy hair, a tribal pressure to add a perfect little brooch. Across the water there is sartorial anarchy.

When the British travel to France and appear in public wearing blue denim with black patent leather, the French stand back in appalled envy. The nerve of us! Have we given no thought to the consequences of teaming grey socks with tan sandals? Are we serious in our proposition that one handbag per lifetime is enough for any woman? And what would become of the world's milliners and dry cleaners, lace-makers, manicurists, pearl-stringers and shoe-tree carvers if everyone went British?

The French find our attitude refreshing. They accept the impossibility of emulating us. They know that a momentary lapse on their part, perhaps a belt or a little scarf that is not quite . . . and they will have their whole reputation to rebuild. Mainly they were taught this by their mothers, who ruled the wardrobe with an iron fist in a hand-stitched Italian calf glove. But their fantasies about wearing Etam head to toe and letting the labrador sleep on it are rich and wonderful.

There are also those French, small in number but vocal and

visible, who cultivate the other British look – pure Jermyn Street. Amongst the *bon chic bon genre* of Paris, to be mistaken for *un vrai Sloane* c'est too much, quoi! It is hard to credit it now, but well into this century rich Europeans turned towards Savile Row when they prayed, and sent their shirts to London to be washed and ironed.

Our faces are different too. In the correct execution of their vowels the French spend many hours a day with their lips pursed or stretched. They have the best exercised zygomaticus muscles in the world. For the British, the counsel of perfection is never to move any facial muscles at all. This is the reason the British speak such poor French.

'Those Onion Johnnies,' sigh the British, 'are so rude, so argumentative, so *suspicious*. You can never make friends with a Frog.' The Frog replies. 'You British, how can you drink warm beer with men you hardly know and call them mates? Talk about the weather for 20 years and call it friendship? Invite total strangers of no more than five years standing into your home and give them dinner?' This touches on a fundamental misunderstanding between two nations. The question is, what *is* a friend?

14

To the British a friend is someone who will be satisfied with a lifetime of banalities and evasions. Brit can know Brit for 30 years without ever revealing his politics, his passions, or the name of his Freemasons Lodge. Anything remarkable he does say will slip out after three double scotches, and not in reply to searching questions. The most direct enquiry one Brit will make of another is 'Been anywhere nice for your holiday?'

When the British ask 'How are you?' the correct response is 'Well, thank you. And you?' This frittering of an opportunity to unfold a full clinical case history baffles the French. If you have had trouble with your kidneys, ankles, and inner ear, if the suppositories didn't work, your surgeon is on holiday, and the osteopath is a fool, why on earth not say so? No one will listen, so there's no risk of future indiscretions, and talking can be so therapeutic. The British cannot agree. They aim to conduct every train journey, illness and marriage in polite silence.

When the French and British meet socially this difference hampers them. The old-fashioned formalities of French *politesse* are used as a foundation for rigorous philosophical argument. They have no fear of conversational roller-coasters. The British, who will slap you on the back, buy you a beer, and call you Dick the very moment they know your name is Richard, prefer to paddle in the shallows. They love set pieces. 'Apparently the holly's got a lot of berries this year . . .' says Dick's friend. '. . . So we're in for a long, hard winter!' finishes Dick. A quarrelsome Brit might chip in with 'Bullshit!' But only a Frenchman would rouse himself to take this bit of teleologic folklore apart and pulverise it.

Our little differences interest the British more than they do the French. Our self-absorption when we're at home becomes fragile abroad. The French have a much stronger sense of their place in the world, a self-confidence that enables them to remark that other people are different and probably inferior, but so what? Legendary British individualism is something they can relate to because they do a very nice line in individualism themselves. They quite admire our scepticism, which is nearly as thorough as theirs. And they feel that with a little practice we might become almost as expert as they are at bucking the system. The French, who have perfected the art of wrangling and fixing, know that the British just write letters to *The Times*.

French women, whose husbands betray them for other French women, feel sorry for British women who share their husbands with Manchester United and stripped car engines. But both have worked out ways of staying married. The French way is labour-intensive and highly competitive. It involves long hours under a hairdryer and absolutely no sisterly solidarity. French wives keep their husbands by being clever and discreet. The British way uses far less energy. It relies on an understanding between British women that their men are all flatulent schoolboys who will never stray far from the chance of a steamed suet pudding. When a British husband does wander, the new woman in his life is not really regarded as a winner. She is seen more as the temporary custodian of a booby prize, and the idea that he may have gone because his wife stopped shaving her legs doesn't arise. It's more likely he's found a girl who doesn't mind him watching snooker during sex.

In other ways we grow closer in spite of ourselves. Brits are starting to eat better. The French are eating worse. The British think culture is something difficult and expensive, the French think culture is three hours a night communing through a Minitel Sex Channel. They had a bloody revolution, we had one that went off at half-cock. Both left us with class-ridden societies. Ours takes few prisoners but does allow Jack the Lad to hobnob with Royalty. Theirs is just plain stuffy.

They are roosters. More precisely they are 54 million different roosters. We are the Bulldog Breed. They crow, we waddle and snuffle. We may needle each other in the way fur and feather sometimes do, but love conquers all. To a bulldog, a rooster can seem rather magnificent. And to all the other roosters too.

To France, Almost

Daytrippers

Every Saturday of the year, in the early hours, and sometimes under cover of darkness, a small invasion force slips anchor from coach stations nationwide and heads for France. Calais and Boulogne and Dieppe don't bother posting nightwatchmen along their Channel coast. They know precisely what they've got coming to them: the British, armed with avarice, suspicion, and very large shopping bags.

Truth is often stranger than fiction. I shall be accused of creative license when I say that some Brits go on daytrips to France and never touch foreign soil, but it is true. I personally know two people who judged it safer to stay on the boat.

Their anxiety is misplaced. Any Shoppers' Trip to France worth its salt will cocoon its participants in snug familiarity and ensure that they arrive back in Chippenham unharmed by Continental vapours. If you wish to, you can hop across, pillage the hypermarket, and never even have to use a hole in the ground. Modern travel can be a wonderful thing.

Most daytrippers go for cheap booze. They say they go for pâté, but pâté is incidental to the main business of bringing home the drink allowance in full, plus a bit more in case of breakages. There are savings to be made, even when you take into account the cost of going there, and the British unease with alcohol is such that they feel driven to have plenty put by. After all, it might disappear. This is especially so during the month before Christmas. There's a lot of drinking to do, and for the 48 hours of Christmas Day and Boxing Day it won't be possible to replenish stocks.

Coach drivers on Shoppers' Trips are quick to reassure their passengers on two important scores. A and 1, the belly of the coach is capacious enough to accommodate everyone's full allowance and some. B and 2, it will not be necessary to tangle with the French language. This sets a cheerful mood for the drive to the Channel ports. The driver is a veteran. He knows all the Frog tricks, won't let any foreign harm come to his flock, and probably won't even have to drive on the right. This man isn't just HGV licensed, he's a master of psychology as well.

'When you get on the boat,' he says, 'you'll find you can use your English money for your coffees and your teas.' He never misses an opportunity to slip in a reassuring possessive pronoun. If you're lucky you can use your English money to buy your lagers as well, for the kind of breakfast so many daytrippers prefer. 'When we get to Boulogne,' he soothes, 'they'll be an hour ahead of the proper time. Don't bother changing your watches. As long as we all stick to the *real* time we shan't have any misunderstandings.'

As soon as the coach wheels touch France, the sense of siege is heightened. The smoke rate increases to Battle Stations. Without a serious fug there's always the risk of glimpsing a wayside Horse Steak Merchant or Snail Throttler. The Chas and Dave tape is turned up loud, lest the sound of Charles Aznavour come floating across the ether. Many trippers simply close their eyes and think of England.

Shopping in a Channel port hypermarket doesn't have to be an alarmingly cosmopolitan experience. If you wish, you can push your trolley straight round to the Serious Hooch Department, pay with plastic, and then eat at one of le fish and chipburger bars outside. If your nerves are stronger you can take a look at some of the rum grub the French live on – fresh vegetables, preserved vegetables, dozens of soft cheeses, thousands of things made from pigs, and of course, that bread

people are always talking about. In fact, you'll only get the slightest impression of what a French hypermarket can be like. Those sited nearest the ports have their eye firmly on the British purse. Faced with the choice of using space for a barrow-load of artichokes or an extra display of Bacardi, the bottles must win.

British daytrippers buy very little wine. Those who do, favour German wine and Italian sparklers, and risk labelling themselves as toffee-nosed show-offs with money to burn. The point of the trip for most Brits is cheap spirits and cheap beer. They cluster around the liqueurs and the designer drinks, arguing about the legal Malibu allowance. They cannot believe how much beer they can afford to take home. More than they can possible carry. You can see the benders and the hangovers taking shape behind their greedy little eyes, and the cry goes out 'They're giving it away! Get 'em in fast!'

It would be as well for France if we went straight from the hypermarket checkout to the ferry, and left nothing behind but our francs. Inevitably, though, there's time to spare. Time to explore, to reel out a bit more of the safety line between us and the coach, and for those of a pioneering disposition, time to risk the local food.

I don't wish to overstate my case. Many British daytrippers manage on sandwiches, and never trouble the *restaurateurs* of Pas de Calais for a pot of tea. There are also Brits who go to Dieppe for a long French lunch and never even consider the savings to be made on lager. But there is a British presence that gets peckish two hours before the boat sails and, having drunk deep at the cup of Dutch courage, decides there's nothing to this franglais lark. Their impudence is embarrassing. The civility with which their needs are serviced is a tribute to French business sense.

Over and over I've watched busy French *patrons* take the time to untangle the warped vowels and glottal stops of a hungry British drunkard. 'Go 'enny crayb may'? Nah, nah, CRAYB, nip nip, know wha' ah mean? Fackin' Nora. Thort this was the fackin' sea side! Wotchergo' if ya aint go' crayb? Steak? Ya go' steak? 'N Chipz? Ya go' chipz. Roit. Weelave three steaks 'n chipz an' three beers pronto. Angon. Tosser's guts is playin' im ap. Wayrz the bog?'

My own French is not proficient at this level. I can do a Languedoc accent, but Fackin' Norette eludes me. So my attempt at turning the tables on ordinary restaurant staff in Dover was hardly fair. I spoke to them in polite French, clearly and slowly. Not only did they not understand me. They couldn't really see why they should. In fact the very idea tickled them pink.

The worst of the tripping Brits is seen by few French. Those who work around the ferry ports do see us drunk, large numbers of men and women barely able to stand. But the most serious session of drinking happens on the boat home. For the first time that day there is a genuine sense of moving in the right direction, homeward bound, away from Abroad, nearer my God to Thee. This is the relieved drinking of people who have proved their mettle, crossed the water, and duped the Frogs out of a whole coachload of cut-price booze. They are beer billionaires! They've been to France, and apart from Tosser they haven't caught anything nasty. They are victors, on their way home with tales of derring-do and a bottle of Pernod. They'd often said they'd like to show Them Frogs a thing or two, and now they have. They definitely have.

Convenient for the Picardy Line

The Channel Tunnel, which everyone says *they're* not going to use, what if there's a fire, think of the risk of rabies, it'll probably never be completed the way the price keeps going up, and anyway ferry strikes and seasickness aren't as bad as they're cracked up to be – that Channel Tunnel – has created an important demographic change in northern France. Houses that French families don't want to live in any more are being bought by Brits who think they may be on to something. Something like being able to commute from Bruay-en-Artois to High Holborn.

Until the mid-'80s the only Brits who settled so near and yet so far from the Kent coast were those who had done something unspeakable – like passing the port the wrong way – and who needed to put a bit of water between their shame and the scorn of the British Establishment. It was like a departure lounge, where you waited to hear whether your flight back to respectable London society would be given permission to land. Those who seriously wanted to live in France headed south.

The British who are now avidly buying every cattle byre in the Pas-de-Calais aren't seeking sanctuary or the sun. They're there because it's cheap.

Those who have already bought, tussle with an internal conflict. Obviously, if you're on to a good thing you don't want everyone clambering on the bandwagon with you. On the other hand, if you've bought a little place for half what it would have cost you in Sevenoaks, it's hard to stop that crow escaping from your throat. 'We see it as an investment opportunity' they say, trying to stifle the greedy tendency to count their chickens before they're hatched. They may be proved right. Or they may find that they have a perfectly delightful seven-bed Norman millstone hanging round their neck. Only time will tell. The important question for now is how fast can they get there, door to door.

Cross-Channel Travel Time is set to become the most tedious topic of conversation of the '90s. It has been tiresome enough accommodating the M25 and the Dartford Tunnel at every dinner party and fork supper. Now we must be prepared to weigh the cost-effectiveness of the hovercraft, and wonder whether anyone in their right mind wants to see how fast they can get from Amiens to Sidcup on a Sunday night. We shall be expected to listen attentively to news of a little-known detour via Caudebec-en-Caux that can shave three minutes off the run to Boulogne, and show our appreciation of men who've got it down to five hours 40 minutes, cattle on road permitting. Gone are the days of the leisurely punt across to Dieppe for lunch. Gone is the possibility of going the *slowest* way, to have time to read a book or fall in love. They've got to get there fast because there's work needs doing on their investment opportunity, and time is money . . . or is it the other way round? And France? Seems quite nice. What they've seen of it.

The ultimate fantasy of the British home owner in France is Mucking In With The Locals. It says nothing whatsoever about the French that this dream withers on the branch if you're only resident in your *fermette* one weekend in four, and are still depending on O Level French *circa* 1963. 'We're on speaking terms with pretty well everyone in the village' does not have the same significance it would have in Sussex. In France everyone says 'Bonjour'. It is an essential prelude to buying bread, passing on the stairs, and probably to mugging someone in a dark alley. It doesn't mean, as it does in England, that a thorough search has been made in Debrett's Peerage and the neighbours are satisfied that you're cut from the right sort of cloth.

The only Brits who even approach the threshold of easy familiarity in France are those who settle there permanently and speak French. Even for them, progress is slow. One of the impediments they must overcome is all the other Brits. A perverse brand of camaraderie is at work in regions where the British are thickly settled. On the one hand, what a relief to meet some really nice people from Orpington who are doing their own re-wiring. On the other, how can one possibly feel pioneeringly cosmopolitan if Clifford and Barbara keep dropping by? What if they too discover that little gem of a cheap and totally authentic local restaurant, and fill it with British friends? Straddling this dilemma, a whole new system of point-scoring is evolving. Arcane snippets of local know-how are shared or witheld, and evidence of genuine social intercourse with the natives is dropped artlessly into conversation, as though it happens all the time. It doesn't.

The novelty of the British buying run-down properties and playing house in them is wearing off for the French. Three or four years ago there was both resentment of Brits who tackled

ambitious renovations themselves instead of paying local tradesmen, and a fascination with their foolhardy courage. Now the French are beginning their own *crise de bricolage*. It is even possible that by the turn of the century a Frenchman will skip lunch so he can finish lagging the loft. Only the crustier elements of *France profonde* will adjust their berets, shrug their shoulders and murmur '*Bande d'idiots!*'

Which is exactly the kind of local colour you want when you've bought a place in France. You don't want people called Pippa organising gymkhanas, or someone you know slightly from Bagshot Rotarians phoning to see if you have any Harpic. You want enquiries from the lady in the *boulangerie* about your children, and a full clinical history of the postmistress' liver.

Eventually you want the whole bang shoot sitting round your scrubbed pine table, reminiscing about '68, arguing about Roland Barthes, and marvelling at your achievements with two stringy partridges and an Electric Crock Pot. Let's face it, you want stick-on peel-off weekend Frenchness. Good bread, cheap wine, and the God-given right to shave your armpits and work in Bromley.

The trouble is, *belonging* doesn't happen this way. You have only to consider the unlikely reverse scenario of Henri and Martine buying the place next door to you for the occasional mooch to the pub and traditional Sunday lunch. If they were ineffably French, as nice as they looked you'd probably decide you wouldn't have much in common with them. And if they tried to act British, you'd think it was a joke, rather sick, and at your expense.

Where a love affair exists at all between the French and the British, for the most part it is one-sided. Brits who take to the French way of things go overboard. They enthuse and flatter and everywhere they turn find further proof that the French possess the secret of the art of good living. The French absolutely agree. They are only surprised that some people have been so slow to realise it, and they are not in the least interested in evidential comparisons. Why should they ever consider the way things are done outside France when they've known since they were in short trousers that France is where it is.

This is why British second-homers do not necessarily endear themselves to their French neighbours by acting Frenchly. To behave sensibly at last is not cause for congratulation. They are pleased when we see the light, but not overwhelmed. And in one respect at least it seems we never learn. We expect familiarity.

The Chunnelling Classes of Britain are also the Entertaining Classes. The Brits who buy places in the Seine-Maritime are the sociable, accessible people who think nothing, when they're at home in Kent, of having people in. They disparage the world of grand dinners and scheming hostesses. They lift the phone and say 'Come to dinner on Friday night.' Just like that. Then they set up kitchen in France and think 'Must get to know the neighbours.' On the basis of an acquaintanceship of less than three years standing, they invite the locals in for food. The locals are charmed. They accept. The evening is a stunning success, in spite of a slip up with the pastry, everyone thaws out, the language barrier is leapt, and the farewells are boozily but genuinely warm. They wait to be invited back.

They wait and wait. Those whose hospitality is returned discover that there is nothing spontaneous, nothing hit-and-miss about a French domestic dinner. The host and hostess will have agonised over the provenance of the meat and the worthiness of the fruit. The perfection of what is offered takes precedence over the willingness of guests to be enchanted by everything. In short, it's not much fun. No great surprise then that the return invitations don't come cascading through the door. The French position is, better to maintain a polite distance than risk offending with an under-ripe cheese.

The British, in their eagerness to become overnight natives and score one over Clifford and Barbara, find this very hard to accept. They take for granted the informality of British social life, of first names and come-as-you-are. The very real prospect that they will never progress beyond Monsieur and Madame with some of their newfound friends frustrates them, and they fail to realise that in France you can set back a relationship several years by rushing. An apprenticeship, a year or two to absorb the hierarchies and *politesse* of the community, would be time much better spent than insisting you know how to play *boules* and then treating it as a light-hearted game.

Friendship is much harder won in France than it is in Britain. Weekend friendships even more so. It shouldn't disappoint us that if we go to another country in large numbers, gobble up property, and still spend most of our time at home, the locals will be briefly amused, and in the long run, uninterested. If we expect them to provide entertaining native colour for our weekend house parties, if we cultivate them to improve our stock as accomplished Europeans and then ask them to make sure our pipes don't freeze while we're spending Christmas in Surrey, is it really any wonder that they think we have a bloody cheek?

Vive La Différence

Twenty Potholes on the way to Entente Cordiale

1 *De luxe* is a French expression, but not a French
condition. The standard of plumbing, heating, and
decorative repair in France is often shocking, even to
the British, reared in the land of malevolent gas geysers
and iron mangles. As a nation the French are not
impassioned by front-loading washer-driers. The word
luxury, in so far as it has any significance, might be
applied to a shower that does not spit damp rust just as
you're nicely soaped. The French for it is *luxe*. The word
luxure means debauchery, in the shower and elsewhere,
and is an excellent reason for never using either word
unless you are very sure of yourself.

2 The handshake is an important part of normal social
relations in France and not just something you do the
first time you meet someone. It is done on greeting and
on parting, between strangers, close relatives, and even
children. It is easier than kissing, commoner than kissing,
and very rude to demur.

3 Kissing is not as much a feature of French life as the
British like to suppose. When it happens, the order is left
cheek, right cheek – exactly the opposite of the air
kissing in British high society. Hand-kissing is done as
much in France as hat-raising in Britain – rarely, and
only by pre-war models.

4 The French eat with forks *and* knives.

29

5 The use of *merci* in response to an offer of something will be interpreted as No.

6 Excretion is regarded in France as the normal outcome of eating and drinking and has never attracted the anxiety that attends it in Britain. Privacy and the maintenance of dignity are not strained after. If there's a door on the cabin, all well and good. If not, a man will inevitably do what a man has to do, and often in mixed company. Separate signs to the Ladies and Gents are not significant. They may merely point out different routes to the same three urinals and open-plan septic tank.

7 French dogs are even less inhibited in their lavatorial habits than their owners. They do it everywhere, but do not use toilet paper, and are then allowed to sit on chairs in restaurants. It is also quite acceptable to beat your dog in France, though not for manuring the boulevard or wiping his shitty little backside all over the seats in Le Procope.

8 It is perfectly polite to *tutoyer* a dog, even if you have never met him before. In all other encounters the O Level French advice that *tu* is fine for anyone under the age of 40 is dangerously inadequate. *Tu* is not just a grammatical form. It is an important but subtle social signal. There are some people you will *never tutoie*, not if the suns falls into the sea and the *Poilane Boulangerie* starts selling Mighty White. There are French people, married for a lifetime, who never *tutoient* one another. It does not necessarily have anything to do with age, pecking order or intimacy. It has plenty to do with respect, and distance, and a preference for good form rather than hurried chumminess. The correct and safe thing to do is to let the French make the first move.

9 The French are formidable letter writers. They write formally and ponderously. The set felicitations are unavoidable because nothing else has been devised, and the hastily scratched card 'Dinner Saturday? Bring a bloke' is just not on. Nor are they converted to the use of perfumed notelets, or any cards very much, except for plain white ones. Christmas card hunting, which opens in Britain on August 12th, has only a modest following in France.

10 So has the offering of wine as a gift. A bottle of Scotch is better. So is a cake. And flowers are perfect, but not red roses, not white lilies, and never chrysanthemums whatever their colour.

11 The French have a more phlegmatic attitude to teenagers and drinking than the British. Alcohol can be served to them in cafés once they are 14, and because identity cards are carried, ages are easily verified. This contrasts strongly with the confusion and cynicism that prevails in British pubs.

12 A French bar is not a pub. If you buy at the zinc you drink at the zinc. Drinking at tables costs more, so you really need to make your mind up about sitting or standing before you order.

13 On the Metro and on buses the designation of a seat for the use of *mutilés* carries more authority than in Britain. If you are lame, halt, or pregnant you can oust the 13-year-old gum-chewer who's occupying your place and expect the moral support of your fellow passengers.

14 French railway stations do not have ticket collectors. They have little orange machines. Any ticket bought in

France that looks small enough to be fed into the machine for date-stamping must get the treatment. Big flapping books of tickets are obviously exempt. But if you get on the train without stamping any other sort of ticket you'll get hauled up by the ticket inspector and fined a supplement. So before you head for the platform, think, take out your ticket, and *compostez-le*! If you break your journey overnight, do it again when you resume your travels, and if you use a bus, remember it may have a little orange machine as well.

15 Never go to bed in France expecting a pillow. You may get one. You may not. In France it is a compliment to say of a man 'I bet he sleeps on a bolster.'

16 A French pedestrian crossing is not the equivalent of a British one. It should be used tentatively, and those whose reflexes are slow, through age or indisposition, should resign themselves to living out the rest of their days on this side of the street. Using a French crossing does not significantly reduce the chances of getting run over, but if you do, and you end up suing, the fact may tilt the case slightly in your favour.

17 If you do get run over you should know that you cannot call an ambulance from a public telephone without putting some money in first. Nor the fire service, police, or operator. Always take the precaution of having a pocket full of small change just in case you get your head stuck in any railings or apprehend any murderers.

18 Failure to carry at least 10 francs worth of currency about your person could lead to your being charged with vagrancy.

19 Some French banks are on the alert against undesirables, vagrants wishing to withdraw 10 francs in used coin for instance, and so keep their doors locked. Having ascertained that you are there during normal banking hours, that it is neither the Feast of the Assumption, All Saints, Armistice, nor one of seven other annual excuses the French find for closing their banks, then comb your hair, straighten your tie, and ring the bell. You will be admitted.

20 In beautiful little French towns the only hotel is often on the beautiful little market square. Secure yourself a very reasonably priced room, enjoy a remarkably good dinner, and sleep the sleep of the innocent. When you wake the next morning and find that a two-day goose market has been erected around your car, console yourself with these two thoughts. Encircling foreign cars with market stalls at first light is an ancient French custom which does wonders for hotel trade and brings a bit of mirth and jollity to the lives of spinach farmers, Senegalese wristwatch vendors, and other noble peasants. Also, it's your own fault for not asking. Stop griping and enjoy the geese.

EURO-BUREAUCRACY: BRUSSELS, STRASBOURG, AND LUXEMBOURG

Living in the House that Jacques Built

France is one thing. Foreign certainly, but we've lived next door to it for ever, niggling and scrapping and peering at it through the Channel mists. Europe is something else. We've had less than 40 years to build up a good head of steaming hostility towards it, with a major interruption in 1973 when we officially became part of it. We still have a lot to learn.

As a prelude to writing about the British in Europe I went out onto the streets of my busy, thrusting home town and asked 20 strangers if they knew the name of their MEP. None of them did. A few were mildly embarrassed and said they had it on the tip of their tongue, but they didn't. Most were unapologetically bored with the question, and with my exciting clue that he had recently become Vice-President of the European Parliament. They couldn't have cared less.

I pressed on. I asked at the library and the librarian didn't know, but she thought I could probably look it up in something. She wasn't sure what. I decided I must be living in a political black hole, so I telephoned acquaintances around the

34

country and asked them the names of their MEPs. Out of 10 people questioned, only one was able to give me an immediate and confident answer. No one else knew, no one else cared. When I told them the answer they didn't jot it down, or say 'Of course! Little round-faced chap. Used to teach Business Studies.' They just said 'Waste of money if you ask me! The Common Market is a total waste of money.'

The idea of a United States of Europe, with Britain part of it, is an old one. Even Ernie Bevin dreamed of being able to buy a ticket at Victoria and just *go*. 1992 should mean that we can live and work anywhere in the Community, trundling down from Denmark for a weekend in Portugal with never a border guard to scowl at us. The whole concept is doomed to make the British feel edgy. We are accustomed to feeling safely tucked in by ocean. An *island mentality* isn't something to snigger about. It's a genuine, visceral feeling of dread that afflicts islanders when they contemplate the vastness of a continent. Once you're on mainland Europe anything might happen. If your brakes failed you could end up in Vladivostok, or China.

The Story of the European Club

When we joined the EEC in 1973, France and Germany had more than a twenty-year start on us. It had begun as a union of their coal and steel industries, to prevent the secret manufacture of guns to waggle at each other. By 1957, Italy, Belgium, the Netherlands, and Luxembourg were in, and there was real progress on a unified nuclear energy policy, and on economic co-operation. At this point Britain didn't ask to join. It started its own club instead. The EFTA Gang (Britain, Portugal, Switzerland, Austria, and the Scandinavian countries) thought it would see off the EEC Gang, but it misjudged the situation.

By 1961 we were asking them to let us in, and General de Gaulle said 'Non!' He kept saying it. We had to wait until he had gone before we could join, and as newcomers we were at a disadvantage to those who'd made up the rules. That's the thing about clubs. If you're not a founder member you have to be patient and work yourself in.

Everyone in what is now called simply the EC complains about it. The dissenting British voice is only one of 12. Those who are employed by it feel frustrated and misunderstood, and the rest talk, in the most self-interested vein, of disillusion and disappointment. 'Nothing but a tribe of paper shufflers!' people cry, though in fact the EC's Civil Service – The European Commission – is quite a slim-line operation. Administering Britain takes 20 times more bureaucrats than does the administration of the EC, and as many as a third of EC employees are translators, keeping the lines open between the speakers of its nine official languages.

Officially, English and French have joint status as the main working languages. Not surprisingly, English predominates. It isn't that the British aren't willing to use French. They are, even when they're talking to the Dutch, who would actually prefer English. The fact that we latecomers to Europe speak the world's most widely understood language rankles with those whose first choice is French. Like us, the French aren't very interested in other people's languages. Unlike us, when they decide to learn a second language, the French make a very thorough job of it.

The British do not yet have a firm grasp of the working parts of the Community. Our prevailing image of the EC is of Jacques Delors baiting us from the top of a butter mountain. We are horribly confused about the Common Agricultural Policy, Strasbourg and Luxembourg, and which side of the road we shall have to drive on in 1992. According to the European on the Clapham Omnibus there's a whole bunch of them, mainly Frogs and Krauts and Eyeties, living the life of Riley somewhere between Belgium and Italy, shouting at the Brits in foreign tongues, envying us our glorious past and forever asking us to put our hands in our pockets.

To be fair, much of this confusion is of the Community's own creation. Its constituent parts are not well-publicised, some of it works in secret, and much of it keeps shifting around in a massive transhumance of politicians and paper.

The European Commission

To begin at the beginning, the European Commission is the place where most Community action is conceived. It lives in the Berlaymont building, a metro-ride from the centre of Brussels, and its Commissioners, who are nominated by each member government, are not elected representatives. Their pedigree doesn't have to be political at all. The British public has great difficulty naming any Commissioners, past, present, foreign, or home-grown, and those who can regard the appointment as a kind of political exile. In British politics there is only one thing more finished than the national career of a newly-appointed European Commissioner, and that is the

career of a former Commissioner. The career path of Pierre Mauroy, who went on to become his country's prime minister, is unthinkable for a British Commissioner.

The image Britain harbours of the Commission – of a dangerous foreign junta – is crazy. We belong to it. We are as much a part of it as every other member nation. What makes us uneasy is the fact that our Commissioners aren't there to shout for us, they are there 'In The Interests Of The Community'. The idea of Leon Brittan and Bruce Millan living it up in Brussels until 1992 on the basis of such an abstract brief seems very rum indeed. Are they actually *doing* anything there? And are they getting fabulously well paid? Well, Yes and Yes.

Commissioners are the instigators and the implementers. They meet in Brussels and say things like 'We really ought to look at the standardisation of banking practice' or 'It's time something was done about dog shit.' They mull these things over. Consult M E Ps and experts in the fields of banking and dog shit. They bring their considerable wisdom and experience to bear on the problems of the day, they make recommendations, and when the new Directive on Canine Excreta becomes law, they supervise its implementation. But they don't *create* the new laws. That is the prerogative of the Council of Ministers.

The Council of Ministers

Commissioners, you will recall, are Europeans first and last. They are committed to consensus and to Community ideals. The Council of Ministers isn't. It doesn't exist in a permanent, visualisable form. When the Council of Ministers needs to talk about lamb, all the national Agriculture Ministers meet. Then they go home and all the Health Ministers check in to talk about heroin. Whenever a Minister decides to spend more time with his family, that particular Council of Ministers has to get used to a new face.

38

The Council meets in Brussels, next door to the Berlaymont, except when it's meeting in Luxembourg, which it does two or three times a year for old times' sake. This is just one example of the extra mileage clocked up to Eurogovernment, because Luxembourg used to be big enough to accommodate Community meetings and is too sore a loser to let go now. They've built a new European Conference Centre in Luxembourg, in defiance of the writing that is clearly on the wall, and like Strasbourg, they're not going to relinquish their grand Euro ambitions without a lot of squawking.

The Council of Ministers is the most powerful of the Community elements. In its various incarnations it makes Community Law. There are two other notable things about it. First, it is fiercely nationalistic, and as a consequence often deadlocked. Second, it meets behind closed doors.

Before a Council of Ministers meets, acres of groundwork are done by Permanent Representatives. They are members of an élite Brussels-based tribe – civil servants, diplomats – who aim to smooth out the biggest lumps and wrinkles and save their respective national government ministers valuable time. Nevertheless, Council meetings often disintegrate into 12 units of knee-jerk nationalism. Worse still, on some subjects unanimity is required. When there's dissent, an agreed majority vote is not always permitted, and so a decision is made not to make a decision and everyone catches the first flight home. Like any 12-headed animal, the Council of Ministers consumes a lot of oxygen and moves very slowly.

The European Parliament

The Community organ that the British have the most opinions about is the European Parliament. This is because every five years we are asked to elect people to go there and represent us, and because it's sometimes on the telly. We are allowed to see it at work because it's a toothless nattering shop, and its business is narcotically boring.

One of the favourite Euro-nuggets of the Brit in the street is that MEPs do nothing and are handsomely rewarded for their trouble. This is inaccurate. MEPs don't achieve legislative miracles because they're not allowed to. That isn't their job. They are paid to advise, lobby, and niggle, and if they don't seem to bring home any booty that's because they're not there to do that either. They're not elected as plunderers and diddlers. They do represent our interests, but not at the expense of the Community ethos. It's hard for us to understand. We're accustomed to bull-baiting between the Reds and the Blues, with Honourable Members calling each other names and cries of 'Shame!' and 'Disgraceful!'

Nor are MEPs big earners. They get the same salary as our national MPs. 'Ah!' says the disgruntled Euro-constituent, 'But what about the perks!' It's true. MEPs do get perks. One of them is to spend their lives shuttling between Brussels, Strasbourg, and the constituency. Sometimes they travel on international missions. Sometimes they even have to go to Luxembourg. The greater part of their working life is spent in the cockpit of Europe, often with the wipers switched on.

Parliament sits, usually one week out of each month, in the Palais de l'Europe in Strasbourg. These are the full sessions, in the debating chamber, when MEPs sit according to their political allegiances and not in national groups.

Strasbourg occupies very little of an MEP's time, and it blends seamlessly with the general landscape of Eurocracy. Strasbourg, Brussels, Luxembourg. All three are full of bankers in raincoats and beggars in shop doorways. All are forested with flagpoles. The emblem of the EC should be

amended. Twelve stars encircling a limp flag. The EEC build-
ings are in the main inaccessible, and built in the style of the
Intimidation School of Architecture. You aren't likely to find
yourself strolling by and say 'Look Walter, a bunch of limp
flags! Let's pop in and say Well Done to our MEP before we
do the Cathedral.'

The bulk of the MEPs' work is done in the Standing
Committees, and they meet in Brussels. Everyone except the
hoteliers of Strasbourg would be relieved to see everything
sited in Brussels. But until that happens MEPs will keep
catching trains and looking up from their paperwork to say
'Mm . . . Metz! Must be the third Monday in the month.'

The British are noticeable in the Euro-Arena the way a
streaker is noticeable at Royal Ascot – refreshingly different,
but peripheral, and doomed. In a sea of men in immaculate
grey wool it is uplifting to spot a blue tie with a brown suit and
know immediately that you have found a fellow countryman.
There is something heart-warming about the shambolic non-
conformity of a British Eurocrat. You somehow want to rush
up to him and sing 'Stay as sweet as you are, don't ever change,
dear!' That ridiculous British prejudice against people who
have their finger nails buffed, the suspicion that a serious mind
and a good hair cut cannot possibly co-exist, run riot in
Strasbourg where there is an international conspiracy to look
snappy and prosperous.

In Brussels, where the majority of Eurocrats come to rest,
the slickness is diluted. At any one time at least half of its
population is foreign. This is largely ignored by the native
Bruxellois. The British head for the south-eastern suburbs,
Ixelles, Woluwe, Tervuren. They have their own schools and
scout packs, football club, and choral society. They have a
childbirth group and a gay group. They have a self-help group

for people getting divorced. If it weren't for the fact that the streets are rather clean and the meat is cut differently, they could almost imagine they were in Leeds.

It is significant that it is still possible to write about our awkwardness in Europe. Spain and Portugal appear to have settled more comfortably into their European role after five years than we have after eighteen. From the start we never wanted to join. At the end of the war the world didn't look the same to us as it did to mainland Europe. We had a Commonwealth and a special friend across the Atlantic, and they all spoke dialects of English. And we didn't get caught up in all those intellectual enthusiasms that took Europe by storm, because the British don't really go in for a lot of cerebral how's-your-father.

We joined in the end because it looked like the smart thing to do, but we're still not entirely convinced. Europe isn't central to our personal or our political thinking. You can spend weeks on end reading British newspapers and listening to British news broadcasts without ever being reminded about where we belong. You can chat over the garden fence and discover the wide-ranging European concerns of the weekend gardener. 'The French get it all their own way. And the Germans. I read they've passed this law, and we're all going to have to scoff our Euro-quota of frogs' legs and German sausage. Disgusting. I blame it all on Ted Heath. And what's going to happen come 1992? Bugger all. Watch my lips. Euro Bugger All.' You can go over there, inspect certain parts of its quietly humming machine, meet your MEP, gaze with pride on a limp Union Jack, and still feel that none of it has anything to do with Britain.

One Over the Twelve

Some EC Facts and Trivia

1 We are the only member country whose libel law places the burden of proof on the defendant, and entrusts the awarding of damages to juries with zeros before their eyes.

2 The British donate more than eight times as much money to the RSPCA as they do to the NSPCC. During the evacuation of a Gulf embassy the nation was relieved to learn that three diplomatic parrots were safe and well.

3 British women are the most adulterous in Europe, but presumably not with British men, who make love least frequently of all Europeans and don't take long about it when they do. The question arises, who are British wives doing it with?

4 We are the Community's greatest drinkers of milk, swallowers of Valium, and buyers of toilet soap.

5 Britain is the only place in the EC where men cannot publicly holds hands without breaking the law.

6 But if they want to, they are free to wear, unfurl, or otherwise display a swastika.

7 British women are the biggest spenders on clothes in the Community.

8 In all other EC countries, disrespectful behaviour during the playing of the National Anthem is a criminal offence. In Britain it is a favourite pastime. This has been blamed on a lousy anthem and the micro-second attention span of the British brain. In fact many countries have anthems that are longer and drearier than ours, but fear of prison keeps the populace loyally humming along.

9 We have a larger proportion of our population in prison than any other EC country. Fewer than a quarter of our prisoners have committed a crime of violence, and none of them are there for hissing during God Save The Queen.

10 More innocent bystanders have been shot by the police in post-war Britain than in any other EC country. In spite of this we are still fondly characterised as the land of truncheons and pointy helmets.

11 Within Europe we are the only nation to have photographs of naked women in our daily newspapers.

12 Britain has the highest divorce rate in the Community, even though it isn't the easiest place to get a divorce.

13 We are the EC League Champions for homelessness, and the size of our cardboard box population is rising so fast that our grasp of this particular European Wooden Spoon is believed to be unassailable.

LANGUAGE

No Understando the Lingo

Joining a long queue of Brits waiting to sign on for evening classes in foreign languages, it's hard to believe we deserve our reputation for ignorance. But we do. It isn't that some of us aren't willing. A few of us are. And it isn't that we lack brain cells, or learning opportunities. Incentive is what we're short of. Three hundred million people speak English as their first language, and on top of that it's the favourite choice of anyone else who needs to communicate internationally on matters of trade, diplomacy, and technology. We are spoiled rotten.

There is nowhere on the beaten track of tourist and business travel that I have ever been where English doesn't appear alongside the local language. In my most panic-stricken, disoriented moments, surrounded by Chinese ideograms, Arab Thuluth calligraphy, or one of the three different ways of writing Japanese, I have always found an English sign or a solicitous native delighted to be able to practise saying 'May I help you?' English has been the working language of virtually every chambermaid, cab driver, carpet salesman, and professional libertine I've ever met, and the only place in the world I failed to communicate with a hairdresser was California, and that was because she had been ingesting noxious substances.

But nothing drives people to learn like necessity, and necessity is what the British are now having to face. The days of Home & Colonial are gone. Our markets are global and, very pressingly, European. If we want to sell something complicated and expensive to the Germans, but expect to do our sales pitch in English, they will probably buy something similar from the Japanese because *they* will have translated the specifications into accurate German. And that isn't because the Germans don't speak English. When the Berlin Wall came down and Germans took to the streets, it was observed by more than one rueful British journalist that the youth of Germany spoke better English than the *youf dahn Peckham*. The fact is that the Germans and everyone else in Europe are tired of humouring us. They wonder why we lack that spark of cultural curiosity that drives other nations to learn languages and open doors on to different ways of being.

Our education system has connived with us in our wilful avoidance of foreign languages. Specialisation starts as early as 14, and until the effects of the new national curriculum start to dribble through – compulsory study of one foreign language for everyone aged 11 to 16 – we shall still have school-leavers who've done no language studies for two years.

The rest of Europe believes that the study of a modern language is an essential, continuing part of everyone's education, including the university students of science, and medicine, and engineering whose British counterparts haven't opened a language primer in years. The idea of a chemistry student still learning his German verbs would have everyone laughing till they fell off their bar stools in British universities. And the proposal that our children should start learning foreign languages *before* their brains get gunged up with Pot Noodle and Mutant Turtles, is dismissed as outrageous, *avant-garde*, and completely out of the question because in Britain it takes teachers six years to persuade children to sit still and open a book.

The older we get, the harder it comes. The grey matter is less willing, and the achievement of the most modern progress carries with it a terrible social burden – the risk of being caught in possession of a foreign language. In Britain a man who is prepared to stand tall and say with pride 'I am fluent in Spanish and intend to learn Dutch' is a maverick soul. With one stroke he is destroying his credibility as a doughty islander, international mouthpiece, and intellectual yob. There's only one thing he can do to worsen his standing in British society, and that is to speak Spanish with a Spanish accent.

We British are not easily worn down. 1992 is certainly going to follow 1991, and as something European may transpire we are making a bit more effort with Business French and Basic German. There are even a few far-sighted show-offs taking classes in Japanese. But we are still being careful not to sound too authentic. A good Italian accent is deeply embarrassing to a Brit. When I first got the hang of the voiced pharyngeal fricative I hid it from the rest of my Arabic class for weeks. And when we speak French we do our best to sound like Ted Heath, just in case anyone we know is listening.

At least *L'Epicier* Heath had a go. Much was made of the fact that John Major was able to become Foreign Secretary, albeit briefly, without any foreign languages. But it was hardly a remarkable appointment. Finding any British politician who can speak anything foreign well enough to do it in public is not easy.

Paddy Ashdown has Mandarin Chinese and Dyak, which is

47

not going to endear him to his voters any more than Tom King's rusty Swahili. Douglas Hurd is fluent in French and Italian, but then he was a diplomat so you have to make allowances. The best anyone else can muster is halting French and shopper's Spanish, and that is much more agreeable to the British public who are less than trusting of politicians who show signs of being brainy or sucking up to foreigners. I cannot report whether Margaret Thatcher speaks anything fancy. She wouldn't tell me. But as having a go in someone else's language inevitably leads to stumbling, blundering, and publicly making a complete fool of oneself, she probably decided to stick to the well-tested British technique of speaking English, very slowly and very severely.

The prospects aren't good. Whatever language we try to learn, we find ourselves years behind English standards in that country. This does nothing for our national pride and dignity, and makes it very hard to get any practice because every dago we meet wants to improve his English. You can't blame him. It is a superb language, and the whole world is in a permanent scrimmage after chances to polish up a few more phrases. We need to be very determined if we're to silence those polygots and make them listen while we murder their grammar. We need role models too, public figures who can talk to Helmut Kohl or Michel Rocard in *their* languages without blushing to the roots of their hair. I've been told that the Queen speaks excellent French. I think it's time more of us heard her do it.

GERMANY

Fair Comment

Frankfurt and Düsseldorf

Germany occupies a unique place in the British pantheon of bogeymen. A large section of our population had their lives changed for ever by the Second World War, and the post-war dream of a United States of Europe, which the French and Germans embraced with relief, has been treated much more warily in Britain. The reunification of Germany has had all our old doubts and fears breaking through the veneer of Europeanism. However preoccupied Germany appears to be with its own problems and the wider European ones, its role as one of our national black jokes seems set to run and run.

There are two German cities that see a lot of the British. They're glad to have us there, reliably faultless in their hospitality. And if they titter about us, they wait till we've gone home and then do it discreetly. In Düsseldorf and Frankfurt, in Trade Fair Country, they get to see a very skewed sample of the British at work.

To have the next International Tube and Pipe Fair marked in

49

your diary can be an exciting prospect. Imagine an Ideal Home Exhibition, multiply it by about a million, and remove all ground-to-air heat-seeking vegetable peeling devices and anything else that isn't strictly speaking a pipe or a tube. Then, site this fiesta of cylindrical conveyances *abroad*. Away from the wife. Hotel rooms. Know what I mean?

There *are* businessmen who go to Düsseldorf to covet other men's pipes and tubes. There are even a few women who do the same. But the purpose of the trip for the majority is simply this – to slip the leash and call it business.

Preparations for a trade fair start very early. Hotels get booked up years in advance and if you don't join the scramble you end up sleeping in Belgium. Then comes a long period of tilling the psychological earth. 'Damn!' he says to his wife, 'we've got that bloody trade fair in Frankfurt in May. Damn!' One more 'Damn!' and he's really blown it. Some men never learn.

At the office it's a different story. 'I think it would be a very good thing if you did the Frankfurt fair this year, Shirley. Could be a good career move. I mean, the secretary of today could be the executive of tomorrow, and a deeper understand-

ing of the technical side . . . Not that it's all graft while we're there. It's a chance, you know, for us all to relax together, have a few drinks, a few laughs. So as far as I'm concerned, if you want it you've got a seat on that plane.' Who could resist? Probably not Shirley, who always wanted to travel.

Dennis has been in tubes all his life. Seventeen years with Wedderburn's Pipe Clamps and Couplings, man and boy. At Heathrow, on his way to Frankfurt, he is at war with himself. Part of him, a greedy, podgy part of him that is tumbling over the waistband of his trousers, wants to go to an airport bar and get whammed. On expenses, naturally. Another part of him wants to score as a seriously-travelled captain of industry.

This is his agony. Should he take himself off in his shiny suit and have a few drinks? Or should rise above such obvious free-loading, buy a copy of the *Wall Street Journal*, and lard his conversation with jaded references to the airport facilities in Buenos Aires? Airport-dropping is a vital element of preening behaviour and trade fair foreplay.

To be *au fait* with the Duty Free in Bahrain and Singapore, to know the visa ropes at Chiang Kai-Shek and the taxi rank wrinkles at O'Hare, all helps to improve a man's merchant cred. And so does studied brinkmanship. Checking in late, buying a toothbrush in an airport shop, and making calls to the office 10 minutes after you should have headed for the board-ing gate are all strategems for impressing on your fellow travellers that what they are dealing with here is a maverick, an original. The Red Adair of corporate boredom.

Düsseldorf is a serious place of work, and is accustomed to a large foreign presence. The North Americans are there. The Japanese are very visibly there. The British, as yet, are mainly visitors. They try to fit a lot in. Just three or four days to eat, drink, advance Shirley's career, and of course, fly the flag. But Düsseldorf is a willing partner. A kind of pricey paradise for carnivorous beer-drinkers out on the toot.

Frankfurt isn't. A convivial night to remember doesn't come easy in Frankfurt. After a hard day wheeling and dealing, the Frankfurters don't hang about in café-bars. They go home to the suburbs as fast as they can. You have to try a lot harder for your fun in Frankfurt, and the British certainly do.

There's something pathetically innocent about our boys when they're over there. They make a lot of noise, manufacture hilarity out of nothing, and they do it all in unapologetic English. First, they drink a lot. It isn't surprising, when all you have to do is stop a passing waiter, when you can claim it all on expenses, and when it'll stop you wishing you were home playing Ludo with the kids. Best of all, there's no need to get bogged down in a fancy wine list. In Germany, when a man says he'd like a beer, everyone understands.

Second, they are all lads together, or possibly all lads plus Shirley, who now has to work out a smart career move that need not involve taking off her knickers. A crowd of British lads – I use the word *lads* to suggest an attitude rather than an age – is powered by hot air. On the trade stands the amount of bluster is inversely proportional to the expertise, and increases still more in the vicinity of an attractive girl with large breasts. There is a lot of very interesting body language on display. Jutting pelvises. Bedroom eyes. Is this any way to sell Hydraulic Hose Assemblies?

The same hot air carries them along Frankfurt's Kaiserstrasse at night. They're not actually desperate for rampant sex, and just as well. What they're desperate for is *evidence* of rampant sex. Stuff to talk about. 'Remember Frankfurt? Whoaaa!'

The Germans are very good-humoured about us. They zip about in superbly understated suits and haircuts and never snigger about the crumpled shambles of the British camp. We look like we never heard of the trouser press or shoe polish. We are attracted to blazers with extra-long sleeves and ties the colour of snot. We drink too much, think too little, fritter our commercial energies on vain sexual fantasies. We call everyone 'Fritz'.

British wives often fret about what goes on at trade fairs. They shouldn't. When a man comes home from Germany and you ask him what he did, believe him when he tells you 'Not a lot.'

Know what I mean?

Six Steps to Getting on in Germany

1 The War. This is no laughing matter. It burrows into the subconscious and sidles to the tip of the tongue. It is actually very interesting to observe how many subjects have oblique military connections. There is, though, an important generation gap. Amongst the young, patriotism is noticeably lukewarm. Amongst those old enough to remember the war or its immediate aftermath there is a willingness to speak of it in general terms, if not with personal anecdotes. Germany's older citizens have had to live first with losing a scrap that they started, and then with the generous solicitude of the Allies in rebuilding Germany. There are a lot of things they feel uncomfortable about, and the therapy of talking sometimes helps. The harshest words I've heard on this episode of German history have come from German lips.

2 *Du*-ing and *Sie*-ing. As in the French system of *tutoyer*, the gulf between the use of the polite *Sie* for *you*, and the familiarly informal *du* is wide and significant. There is only one safe course of action and that is always to use *Sie*. Using *du* prematurely or inappropriately is as offensive as digging the Queen in the ribs and calling her Liz.

3 Another manifestation of correct form in this most democratic of countries is the importance attached to professional titles and their place in the meritocratic scheme of things. It is as essential to remember someone's title as it is to remember his name. It is more important to remember his surname than his first name, which you will

probably not use during the first 10 years of your relationship.

4 A German's home is his private castle and business entertaining happens elsewhere. Sometimes it nearly doesn't happen at all because a Brit is waiting for a German to offer him dinner, and the German is waiting for the Brit.

5 Tipping, accepting tips, asking for a discount, and generally talking about money comes naturally in Germany. It is not the embarrassing subject we mumble and fumble about in Britain. If someone does you a favour or a service they're not professionally employed to do, like loosening your wheel nuts or rescuing your cat, a small financial token of thanks can change hands in Germany without anyone getting hot under the collar.

6 The British way – whining about red tape before eventually succumbing; thrashing about on the horns of bureaucracy and then complaining that They never get anything done; calling in favours, pulling a few strings, and, if push comes to shove, writing to *The Times* – is not the German way. Germans go by the book.

And Six More to Make Your Day
Go with a Swing

1 Germans shake hands but don't kiss. They shake hands approximately 10 times more often than the British, and

are deeply disapproving of those tonsil-hoovering kisses the British do in public when they think they're in love.

2 Get up in the morning. The German day starts early and doesn't let up. You should aim to be ready for lunch by 12.30 latest.

3 Germans are dedicated users of the clothes brush, shoe polish, and the comb. Also of trouser presses and coat hangers. If your overcoat is a late sixties Army Surplus duffel, with elbow patches and a ripped lining, don't wear it to do business in Germany. It will be noticed, not least because someone may try to help you into it as you prepare to leave. This is common practice and is merely a friendly gesture.

4 A less friendly gesture involves one finger. It is that kind of forehead tapping that is an innocuous British way of suggesting that someone is a brick short of a load. In Germany it is a very rude thing to do. Ruder than two fingers in Britain. So rude, a policeman may caution you.

5 This gesture may be made at you by the cyclist who just ran you down. You thought you were on a footpath. He knows he was on a lane of the footpath designated for cyclists. Beware. In Germany footpaths are not always what they seem.

6 Go Dutch. As in 'If you give me 15 Deutschmarks, Hannelore gives you 60 pfennigs, and I give the waiter 28 marks 50, we still shan't be straight.' This rigmarole is preferred to one person paying for everything, and someone else paying the next time.

GESTURES

Sit on That

The British are not a gesticulating nation. It has been observed by many travellers that the frequency of arm-flapping increases in direct proportion to the nearness of the Mediterranean, and that if you want your shoulder dislocated by way of greeting you must go to the United States. The normal mode for manual extremities in Britain is stationary. We are not great hand-shakers or kissers, though we're supposed to have taught them both to the French, and bowing is done only in very restricted circumstances.

Nonetheless we do have our little mannerisms. Some of them have been adopted by the rest of the world, some can provoke international incidents. One or two transmit such a subtle message that only your best foreign friend might tell you.

A good example of body language quietly giving the wrong impression is the way British men sit and how it is perceived by Americans. In North America *real* men favour the ankle-knee leg cross. This occupies more body space than crossing the legs at the knee or the ankle, and signals that the man believes, or perhaps just hopes, that he's worth so much space. This interesting postural detail has crossed the Atlantic, and British men will do it, particularly if they have something to sell, but it is a long way from being generally adopted and can actually arouse hostility in Brits who don't want to look at a beige nylon ankle sock and seven inches of sparrow's leg.

So when British men go to America and sit around with their legs crossed at the knee or the ankle what does America think? Well it's not so much a thought, as a niggling bad vibration. The suspicion crosses America's mind that British men are pansies.

Our three favourite gestures involve fingers only, probably in the interests of energy conservation. No sense in wearing thermal vests if you're going to dissipate all that bodily warmth in an extravagant display of arm-flailing. The three gestures are Pointing, Beckoning, and, top of the charts for the twenty-third year running, the Two Finger Jerk.

Pointing is not a gesture that travels well. Margaret Thatcher was a great user of the hectoring digit and someone really should have told her. Pointing with a finger to show directions is not really done in South America, black Africa or in Arab cultures. Otherwise it's all right. Pointing, jabbing, and wagging a finger during a discussion is widely read as bossy, threatening, or openly hostile.

Beckoning is not so much offensive as open to confusion. Brits beckon with the palm facing up. So do the French, although the French are less likely to beckon with a single finger. They mainly beckon with the whole hand, and reserve the single finger treatment for children and animals. The Spanish, the Italians, the Japanese, and Arabs beckon with the palm facing the floor, so beckoning Brit-style will either be disregarded because it doesn't mean anything, or it may get loosely translated as something phallic and obscene. In Italy it will be completely misunderstood because there, beckoning with your palm up means Goodbye.

58

It is important to distinguish between the Two Finger Jerk, the Forearm Jerk, and the Winston Churchill Fork, Orthodox and Reversed. Various manifestations of finger jerks and arm jerks have a long history as gestures of insult and sexual innuendo. There is a theory that the British got the finger jerk from sailors and merchants who had toned down a graphic Arab obscenity involving the nose and two fingers. Whatever the truth of its pedigree, the finger jerk delivers a priapic message. The forearm jerk does the same, only bigger. In France where it is widely used, the gist of it is 'Why not move out of my immediate vicinity and go about your business.' The British are more inclined to use two fingers for that, and use the forearm jerk to signal, one man to another, 'Cor, get a load of that!'

Sir Winston's podgy two-fingered V is only 50 years old, but it has captured the world. It is recognised everywhere as a symbol of triumph and fortunately for the travelling Brit is not distinguished from its reversed form, the All-Purpose Two Finger Insult Without Jerk. This means that when the British abroad try to insult some passing road hog, they do not always succeed. Indeed they may receive a friendly Winnie in reply.

Another rich source of embarrassed confusion is the Thumb and Forefinger Circle, used in refined British society to show that something is 'Simply divine'. British politicians sometimes use it to draw attention to the exquisite perfection of their policies, and British businessmen who've taken to American ways now use it a lot to say 'Great! Fine! O K!' Sadly, this does not travel well. To the French it means 'Zilch'. To the Japanese it means 'Money'. And to most Mediterranean and Arab cultures it means 'Bugger me, please bugger me' or, 'I have reason to believe you are a sodomite.' It is not a prudent gesture to cultivate unless you do travel in search of anal intercourse.

There are some gestures that are acceptable everywhere except one place on earth and if you use them there you're a dead man. In Greece an open-handed thrust is a very terrible thing indeed. It is the sort of gesture an unknowing Brit might make to repel some quayside purveyor of sponges or worry beads, not realising that there is only one worse move he could have made. And that is the two-handed thrust.

On Sardinia the problem is different. Thumbs up. It doesn't mean 'Good', and it doesn't mean 'Please motorist stop and let me ride in your car.' In Sardinia a raised thumb is an invitation to sit on it. If it's a lift you need, try waving. If it's local colour you're after, an erect thumb will do nicely.

Finally, though the British don't travel much to Central America as yet, those who are now venturing to Acapulco and Cancun should know this. The Mexican Crotch Scratch is not the same as the British Fly Fumble. The British form carries two meanings. In the rare event of hot weather it may signal 'My nylon Y-fronts are giving me trouble.' More likely though the message is 'Just checking my tackle.' The Mexican form is unambiguous. It means 'Hey, wait till you see what I've got in here!' Men travelling with British passports and itchy underwear should be very cautious indeed.

ITALY

Venus on the Half Shell

Tuscany

Italy has one of the oldest tourist industries in the world. It feels very relaxed about it. Some places have manganese deposits. Some have natural gas. Italy has olive groves, ranked cypresses, Brunelleschi, Giorgione, and thousands of small but perfect churches, which it regards as milkable natural resources. Italians don't really understand why we travel so far to look at frescoes, but now we've pointed out to them that they are living in Aladdin's Cave of Art Treasures, they are happy to charge us for a peep. They wonder why we get solemn about it. They wonder why we read guide books and then worry whether we read the right guide books. And they wonder how much we really enjoy the Italian Experience. As though we went there to enjoy ourselves!

In a sense we treat everything we encounter in Italy as an amazing artefact, designed to be aesthetically at one with the food, the wine, and the sunshine. The few Italians we have any

61

contact with – shopkeepers, villa housekeepers, gardeners with special responsibility for swimming pool maintenance – are all Real Characters. This is a land apparently devoid of boring, unremarkable people who can't cook, sing, form a government, or look like they stepped straight off an Uccello canvas. The British go to Lucca for three weeks and touch the very soul of Italy. They believe.

Usually, when the British travel, they are put out by the foreignness of Abroad. They hang around in beleaguered English-speaking clumps and long for a cup of tea. In Italy, and in particular in Tuscany, it is quite different. There the British despise all other Brits except the members of their own house party. The most vocal complaints about the souvenir mug-buying hoi-polloi who do Florence in a morning come from the British, who absolutely know that a lifetime wouldn't be time enough to do Florence, not from the Florentines, who are philosophical about the wages of tourism.

The British caste system has been transported intact to the fields of Arezzo and Montalcino, and the pecking order, in roughly descending degrees of nobility, is as follows. Aesthete, Art Historian, Rich but Dotty Opiner, Writer, Artist. And, in ascending order of undesirability, Television People, Ruthless Young City Tykes, and Property Hyenas – in fact anyone who has become rich too recently to be able to relax about it, or who is likely to get a fax machine put in.

You don't *buy* into the British Scene in Italy. At best you inherit it, at worst aspire to it. And if you are prudent you spend your time on the waiting list studying, because if the call ever comes you will need to know your Desiderios from your Luca della Robbias . . . 'I can't draw a straight line myself, but I know what I like' will not get you a second invitation to dine in San Gimignano.

There is something apposite about the British, who don't like to complain about anything, invading Tuscany, where there is nothing to complain about. The only thing to mar the idyll is the philistine grunting of the masses. The word has got out, heaven knows how, that there are sights to be seen in Florence. Ghiberti's bronze Baptistery doors, Brunelleschi's Duomo of the Santa Maria del Fiori, the modestly-hung *David* of Donatello, the Santa Croce frescoes of Giotto, the Lippis, the Raphaels, and the ample Rubenses, lolling around as a challenge to anorexic posterity and Weight Watchers International. Also the shops, where you are spoilt for choice in the matter of leather wallets; the close encounters with speeding Vespas and falling masonry; and the inconclusive street corner flirtations with men who love sex, especially standing sex with foreign women, but unfortunately have to be home in time for dinner.

The British culture vultures would have liked Florence to stay the way she was, and she might have done, if they hadn't gone on about it so. Write one book too many on the umber perfection of a place and the coach parties are sure to arrive soon after. The Florentines didn't mind. In fact they were quite keen to put in car parks, Burger King and a dolphinarium. But

the Quattrocento Mob, the Caravaggio Gang, the Mannerist Brigade protested like it was their very own backyard. When the Italians pointed out that being the curators of the world's greatest art treasures needn't stop you earning a fast buck, that you can't actually eat a Leonardo, the British deserted Florence in disgust. They took to the hills, and they now have the treasures of the Tuscan hill towns as comprehensively catalogued as they first had the Uffizi and the Bargello. Only this time they're only letting on to the Right Sort of People.

The Right Sort of People don't just remember the difference between the *Rucellai Madonna*, the *Madonna of the Meadow*, *Madonna and Child with the Young St John*, *Madonna and Child with Four Saints*, *Madonna and Several Saints but No Child*, *Madonna on the Rocks*, and *Venus on the Half Shell*, *No Saints or Children*. They also have fierce allegiances. Some believe Masaccio was an artistic revolutionary in his own right, others think he was predictably derivative of Giotto. Groupies of Piero della Francesca don't give a fig for Bramante. They all know their brushwork. They know their colour and composition. And all firmly resist the suggestion that those pictures and statues are merely quite nice in the flesh, nearly as nice in reproduction, and a lot nicer for the passage of time and the patina of grime.

Cognoscenti is one of the rudest words Italians use when they speak of the British, but of course not all Brits in Tuscany are there to defend the reputation of the Renaissance. Some are there to write, a few with nerve are there to paint, and many are there to find themselves. They are living the kind of mock-pastoral dream that's so hard to achieve in Britain because of the smell of damp beds and the price of extra virgin olive oil.

With the sun on your back, Pisa airport 23 miles away, and maid service included in the price it's not difficult to play at being in touch with the earth, and wonder how one ever existed without bunches of fresh basil.

And when Browning and Ruskin begin to pall, there are always the swimming pool, tennis courts, congenial British friends, and the eternally fascinating gnarled and weathered local peasantry, who till the earth, worry about overheads, and cannot understand why anyone would travel 900 miles to see Segromigno Monte. Perfect living demonstrations of the truth of that old adage, 'Travellers narrow the mind.'

Old Tars Together

Venice

The British and the Venetians are historical soulmates. Both rose from the waves, sailed the oceans, bought short and sold long. Both nose-dived. Venice did it in the 18th century, Britain held on till the 20th, but we were heading in the same direction. Becoming museums.

There our differences begin. The British love visiting museums, but they're not very interested in running them successfully. It is nice to take a foreigner's money as long as he's not after anything too fancy. For instance, we can do basic St Paul's, with copious references to the Royal Wedding, no problem. As for clean lavatories, good cafés, and a willing band of polyglot guides – who wants to pay for that kind of luxury? And if you stop some scurrying native in Paternoster Square and ask the way to St James Garlickhythe, you're likely to be told 'Search me. I'm from Chigwell.'

In Venice everyone is a part-time tourist guide. Being able to direct people to San Zanipolo is as much a part of daily life as breathing. So is shouting picturesquely in Venessian and in-

venting a thousand charming ways to separate visitors from their money. Venice is really in the business. It doesn't feel degraded or shamefaced about it. Venetians cram into St Mark's Square to feed the pigeons. And they love riding in gondolas. It's not the Venetians who want to get away from all the tourists. It's the British.

Venice appeals to the British on two fronts. First, it is filled to the rafters with *important* art. Second, it is an excellent location for getting romance over and done with. This makes it especially inviting for British men who know that romance is a medicine every man has to swallow sooner or later, and who rather like the idea of a brief, expensive blitz which will keep things chipper on the catering and laundering front for years to come. Many of them have confided to me, 'We're just here for three nights. The wife's idea, y'know. Second honeymoon kind of job. Do these gondola chappies really charge as much as they say?'

Art is much more serious. British couples in sensible shoes can be heard laying their battle plans over breakfast. 'Tuck in Edgar. I'd have that other brioche if I were you. We've got a good few Tiepolo ceilings to do before lunchtime.' They visit the Accademia and show themselves no mercy until they've carried out a thorough reconnaissance of all 23 rooms. All of which does nothing to put a dent in I Frari and the San Rocco. Venice doesn't have much night life, and it's just as well. The British prefer a quiet night in with a much-thumbed copy of John Julius Norwich.

The worst blow you can deal a seasoned British visitor in Venice is to show him you know the place as well as he does. Americans want to see St Mark's and get the hell back to the cruise liner. But the hoarding of little hidden architectural gems is a favourite British occupation, even though in Venice there is no such place as Off the Beaten Track. To know where to find Strozzi's *Saint Sebastian* – San Benedetto, second altar on the right – is pretty basic stuff. To be on first name terms with a clam-fisher from Burano is a very big deal indeed.

In 1966, when the floods made everyone realise what structural trouble Venice was in, the British responded with generosity and vigour. They still are. Peer inside the educated British mind and one of the first things you will find is a WRVS uniform, coiled· and ready for action. The Venetians were gratified by our response and glad to have our money. Sadly, there weren't many detailed plans as to how it should be spent. Now Venice is pleased to announce 'We are no longer sinking' and the British note sourly, on their way in from the airport, 'There's a lot of pointing up needs doing.'

Whenever I say I'm off to Venice someone says to me 'I've never been. Does it smell?' It does. There's no denying it. To my nostrils, so do London and Birmingham. Venice is bathed in its own sewage, Britain wades through the *ordure* of chip bags, dog shit and used condoms. Still, there are many Brits for whom their first visit to Venice will be their last. Their nostrils cannot take a smell that is so frankly organic. The Titians may be divine, and the *fegato con polenta* irreproachable, but when all is said and done they prefer Babbacombe.

Venice is on her last legs. Everyone says so. But there are many who also believe that Britain is about to turn belly up. The thing is, Venice is dying much more beautifully, even if you face the petrol refineries at Mestre when you look at her. Her shipyards have closed, her warehouses haven't seen any silk or cinnamon in years, she's got too many crumbling stone lions, too many rich foreigners, too few natives who can afford the rent. She's had it. We've had it. But she's still dressing to receive her admirers.

When in Rome

How to Behave in Italy

It's very easy to get by in Italy because the Italians are the most accommodating of people. When the British do stumble there, it's usually to do with food, or that most fundamental of Italian concepts, *bella figura*.

1 Churches are places of worship. They are not theme parks. I don't know why this still needs to be said, but it does. Shorts, singlets, ice-creams, and men with nothing on their chest but a Pentax are not welcome in Italian churches even when there isn't anything going on. If you want to hear Mass, nothing could be simpler or more informal. You can walk in or out as you please, and unlike Sunday Matins in Cheam, you needn't worry that you're Sitting In Someone's Seat. Just remember to do up your shirt.

2 Speak up. To Italian ears, the British are mute. Our shouting and singing apparatus has dwindled, through lack of use, to a vestigial squeak box. And not only that. We forget to slam doors. We miss opportunities to rattle crockery. And we never do anything after midnight in case it wakes the people in the next room. The Italians feel obliged to make up for the crowds of us who shuffle through their country in silence. They do this by banging their dustbins together at first light. Only complain if you are willing to do it loudly and in the vernacular, and from the safety of a sixth-floor bedroom window.

3 Italian shops open in the morning, close for a long lunch, and open again later in the afternoon. In northern Italy offices now tend to work 9 till 5. In the south, 9 till 1 and then 3 till 7 still prevails. Italian banks close for lunch and stay closed. This can be an unpleasant discovery on a Friday afternoon.

4 Older public phones in Italy take tokens – *gettoni* – instead of cash. The tokens circulate freely as part of the national currency, and if one turns up in your change no one is trying to swindle you. A token is good for 200 lire.

5 Don't look hopefully at the waiter and say 'Erm . . . Pasta?' He will want to take your order in full, and in Italy pasta isn't served in a rib-sticking mountain that will lay you low till morning. It is served as a prelude to something else. A little pasta, followed by a little meat or fish, followed by something vegetable, followed by something sweet. This order of service is a canon of Italian life and is not negotiable. If you want to eat just one course, go to a pizzeria.

6 Drinking coffee in Italy is not the equivalent of drinking tea in Britain. It is much richer in variety. To ask for 'Coffee?' in Italy is about as helpful as asking for 'A drink?' How do you want it? Precisely how? The nearest approximations to British coffee-drinking experiences are *caffèlatte*, which is the kind of gentle, milky brew you might get in one of our department store cafeterias, and *caffè lungo*, which is an ordinary straight black coffee. The two things the British are most inclined to order – *cappuccino* and *espresso* – can spell trouble. Frothy *cappuccino* is only considered suitable as a sort of liquid breakfast. If you order it at the end of a meal the waiter will probably throw up at the very idea. And an *espresso* is a train which doesn't go particularly fast and stops at quite a lot of places. It can also mean a tiny cup of strong, black coffee, but that is just as likely to be called *caffè*. A thimbleful of even stronger coffee is called *caffè ristretto*.

7 Lavatory is *il gabinetto*, but it is not very *bella figura* to ask for it so bluntly. The Italian euphemism, even in public places, is *il bagno*.

8 If an Italian addresses you as *Dottore* it doesn't mean he's going to ask you to lance his boil. He is gracing you with the academic title just in case you can give claim to it. It wouldn't hurt you to follow his example.

9 *Ciao* is the one Italian word all Brits know. Unfortunately it is not an easy word to use. It can be quite inappropriate to the occasion or the relationship, and as the safest course is always to err on the side of formality it wouldn't be a bad idea to leave *ciao* at home.

71

10 When an Italian says 'You must come to my home for dinner' he usually means that he wants you to dine at his house, and soon. The colloquial English translation into 'Farewell. Probably for ever' does not apply in Italy. Nor do strict punctuality, gifts for the host, conversational reticence, and thank you letters the next morning. In this situation *bella figura* means dressing on the formal side, drinking moderately, and above all, joining in.

HOOLIGANS

Not Really Cricket

During the writing of this book Italy was bracing itself for the 1990 World Cup, and the arrival of England's notorious football fans. The point was clearly made that it was the behaviour of the English they feared, not the Scots, and certainly not the Irish.

The Italians are no strangers to football violence. Fierce racist battles between the fans of the northern clubs and those of the south are commonplace and increasing. Nonetheless, the Italian police considered it wise to work closely with British police, and to prepare thoroughly for the invasion. They banned sales of alcohol on match days; deployed thousands of *carabinieri* to segregate and search English fans; borrowed English police to help spot and weed out known ringleaders. They expected the worst.

Meanwhile, the European football season was being played. In Holland the thuggery between some home teams was so bad that their matches were banned; in Germany, East and West, there were riots and running battles. France didn't do too badly, apart from a fire started deliberately in a stand, but Belgium and Italy had regular trouble, Yugoslavia took a nosedive, and Greek matches were abandoned in a fog of tear gas. Even Switzerland had its moments. The British, it seemed, are not the only bad boys in Europe. What they most definitely are is the symbol of badness.

Two things set the British hooligan apart from his European brother. One is his immensely imitable style. The other is his willingness to travel great distances in pursuit of his trade. There is a professionalism about the British yob that the novice thugs of Europe find inspiring. These are not frustrated victims of the class struggle, and they are not the neglected underbelly of Thatcher's Britain. You have only to add up the cost of a weekend in Stockholm getting whammed to see that a typical supporter of the Neanderthal Tendency is a lad with money to burn.

He's in his 20s, employed, and likely to be living at home with his Mum. He quite likes football, but prefers it when it's spiced with the prospect of a ruck. And he collects scars and criminal convictions like awards for valour. On a different throw of the dice he might have become an avid train spotter. The question is, why on earth did he turn out the way he did?

A factor that recurs in all reports of British hooligans abroad, footballers and holidaymakers alike, is booze. Too much, drunk too fast, and an attitude to public drunkenness that verges on the admiring. In Britain, getting drunk is a very significant way of becoming a fully-fledged member of the male tribe. In fact, camaraderie between British males is most unlikely to blossom at all without some serious lubrication.

We are not the world's heaviest drinkers but we are amongst the most illogical. Drinking to the point of throwing up, falling down, or passing out is considered normal; declining alcohol is not. We make drink available to those who want it pretty well any hour of the day, and yet we fall on it as though we may never get our hands on a bottle again. Craziest of all, we drink in teams. In Britain, a man who tries to duck his round is a social pariah. I buy a round. You buy a round. Bill buys a round. And then if George is still standing, *he's* got to buy a round. It is a very effective way of making sure I'm as pissed as you are, and it does have the knock-on benefit that we can all talk tosh together. This is the drinking climate in which young British males learn about solidarity and belonging.

Drink is only part of the story. There is something else going on inside our travelling hooligans. Something brutal and raw. It is as though they are driven by an insistent physical urge to have a scrap.

Is it their diet? Aren't they getting enough exercise? Has it anything to do with lead pollution, poisoned water, or ultra-violet radiation? Or has something terrible assaulted the nation's soul? Do we need a few sessions on a psychiatrist's couch? I think we probably do.

The British boys who go abroad with knives and baseball bats are mad about something. They know that the British flag, the English language, fair play, and a never-setting sun used to be admired and envied the world over. They now know in their hearts that we have fallen on hard times. They don't want to admit it, but if they're forced to admit it then they want

someone to blame. Here lie the roots of their behaviour on foreign streets. Bravado, defiance, and the waving of the Union Jack on behalf of all pure-bred white Gentile Brits. They are our ambassadors of racial hatred and they are one of our most successful exports.

Set-piece battles planned in advance have been one of our gifts to international football. So has the English language. In Germany and Italy many gangs have adopted English names and English war chants.

Our language is the language of pop culture, so whatever young Brits take up, the world soon hears about it. Our inverted snobbery makes a virtue out of ignorance, so our 16-year-olds leave school able to grunt and drink lager. And we have allowed the high-profile, low-forehead fascist movement to capture our flag, so the Union Jack, in vest-form, banner-form, or simply draped around the shoulders of a drunk with a meat cleaver, has taken on a symbolism that used to be reserved for the swastika.

Football hooliganism is not a British disease. We simply perfected it.

CHILDREN

Suffer Little Brits

The world has a macabre interest in how the British have achieved so much in the field of international yobbery, and so little in education. Clearly we must be doing something unusual with our children. We stand charged with benign neglect and militarily planned cruelty, and the only thing said in our favour is that we don't *officially* sanction sweated infant labour and minors living in cardboard boxes.

Our well-tested methods of taking small children away from the motherly bosom and replacing it with the bleak prospect of dormitories, housemasters, and a harsh educational regime, attracts horrified protests and fascinated interest. Many Brits who've survived the system believe it is the fount of that great mobility and inventiveness that used to be so admired in us: young men who knew there was no point in hanging around because big brother was set to inherit the family pile, who set off at a tender age to seek their fortune.

The Italians and the French and the Spanish would understand our banishing of small sobbing boys a lot better if it turned them into magnificent specimens of manhood. But it doesn't. It turns them into men who are awkward with women, stroppy with foreigners, and very, very suspicious of anyone who didn't go to their school. Perfect for the Indian Civil Service. A handicap in modern Europe.

We don't do a lot better with children who escape the boarding school routine. If we ask too much of the ones we send away, we apparently ask too little of the rest. Our state education system, meddled and fiddled with since the '50s, graduates thousands of children every year who can't read, write, or work out the cost of a Double Cheeseburger and a Giant Pepsi. Set alongside this grim and shameful fact, the occasional flap over our teaching of foreign languages seems less important. It is regrettable than more of our teenagers don't have good German. That many German teenagers have better English than British teenagers is almost too painful to admit.

Little Germans are no longer expected to bow or click their heels in the presence of adults, and stoicism isn't as much prized in the kindergarten as it was 30 years ago, but they still turn out with a sounder grasp of more skills than little Brits, and with a notable self-possession.

Somehow the middle course, of being parents who are concerned, affectionate, *and* demanding, has been missed by the British. The Japanese, who are interested in how we do things but not always impressed, have adopted a rigorous version of it. Their small children are caressed, cosseted, snuggled, smothered, and generally over-indulged. Then they go to school. There they are introduced to concepts like sustained endeavour, humility, and failure. They toddle into the system convinced that the sun only rises for the pleasure of shining on them, and emerge from the sausage machine as biddable, serious-minded gatherers of straight As. Japanese school children are just like British school children used to be 40 years ago.

What the Japanese wonder is why did we get bored with having polite and literate children. The Americans wonder something else. They don't understand why our children are so diffident and silent. They don't get the way we dilute any suggestion that one of our kids may have talent. And they really do wonder why more of us don't get those teeth and jug-ears fixed. To the American, for whom everything in life is open to improvement, British children present a frustrating challenge. If only those children were theirs, they'd soon have a coach or two licking them into shape.

Children in Britain who can hold up their end of a conversation with adults and give a good account of themselves are rare. They attract derision. Children who introduce themselves confidently and clearly, or who can order their own dinner in a restaurant are not considered attractive. 'Precocious little sod', everyone murmurs, relieved that they have normal children who slide under the table with a Mutant Turtle instead of reading the menu, and greet anyone who profers them a hand with a thump in the solar plexus.

A fast way to lose friends in Britain is to have prize-winning children, free of bed-wetting, skin complaints, school phobias, tone deafness, adenoids, and a criminal record. When at home, if your children are not flawed, it has a socially lubricating effect to invent some minor impediment. This contrasts starkly with the United States where getting rid of minor impediments is big business.

Americans are appalled by our attitude to parenthood. 'Why have children', they wonder, 'if you're not willing to parade them before paediatricians and tennis coaches and diet counsellers?'

Before you take your children to the United States, best to practise the art of mega-hype. Explain to them about standing

tall, speaking up, and honouring the flag. Tell them that though you usually train the spotlight on their every blemish, in Boston you will massage their batting average and fib about their science grades. They must be warned. Otherwise they will really embarrass you. They'll interrupt your hymn of praise to say 'Dad! Dad! I thought I was a destructive little moron?'

Plainly, as a nation we don't admire our children. We don't even seem to like them very much either. We avoid them like the plague. Apart from the United States, where dinettes and fish finger dinners were invented so that the kids could press on with their heavy schedules, the rest of the world seeks the company of its children. So much so that they even eat with them. British travellers to the Mediterranean like hotels that offer Early Junior Teas. These enable them to keep their children up and on the go right through the heat of the day, so that by five in the afternoon they have become peevish and insufferable and with any luck will sleep while their parents enjoy an evening of serious drinking.

In France, and Italy, and even in Spain where dinner is late, children and adults eat together. That is why their children eat grown-up food, and in Britain, men old enough to be Cabinet Ministers eat nursery slop. We are seen as being neglectful of one of the most precious opportunities of parenthood – to educate our children without their really noticing.

Children who eat in adult company pick up all kinds of things. Tastes, techniques, ideas. Patience too. British children treat a meal as a speed trial. The test is to see how fast they can do Sausage, Chips, and Peas, Fruit Jelly and Non-Dairy Topping, and get back in front of the telly. Not so much a meal, more a pit stop. Around the Mediterranean where they are fighting their own rearguard action against microwaved dinners and compulsive viewing, the battle is thought worth the effort. If you love people, surely you eat with them? If dinner is good, doesn't everyone want some? And if your eight-year-old son cannot sit with you now, tell you his news, mess with his spinach, talk with his mouth full, and be hungry for apple pie but not for bread, what hope is there when he's 18?

In Spain I saw 10 members of one Spanish family dining by a hotel pool. Two of them looked very old, and two others were so small only their hands kept appearing over the table edge. Around them British parents were drinking. Some of them had left their children asleep, five or six floors up. Some of them had failed in the attempt and allowed them to tag along. They bought them drinks. When the snack bar opened up they bought them chips. But there was no place for them at the table. They were an encumbrance to an evening of pleasure. I wasn't the only one who noticed those little British bar-orphans. The Spanish noticed too. They shook their heads and wondered why Stephen and Ashley were mooning unsupervised by the deep end, instead of being petted by Abuelita and finger-fed on prawns.

Notes for the Travelling Parent

1 Allow your children to live by the ticking of the local clock. They will adapt to it fast, and then so will you. Fierce heat, siestas, and long cool evenings go together like fish and chips and . . . more chips.

2 Most British children are fair-skinned and most British parents fail dismally to protect them from the sun. Mediterranean people are horrified by the way we allow our children to fry. Cover them, head to toe. On the beach, in the water, and on coach trips that start after breakfast and don't finish till the evening. Just cover them.

3 Don't drag your children screaming along foreign streets, and don't cuff them, insult them, or send them packing in public. Other nations treasure their children.

4 The British assume every dog is innocent until proven guilty, and pass this attitude on to their children. When abroad, assume every dog rabid until proven muzzled, and tell your children to pat *nothing*.

5 Trust your children to make their own decisions about food they haven't seen before. Any child raised on British sausages, baked beans, and blackcurrant cordial has a stomach of iron.

6 Colouring books, Actifed syrup, a strong restraining strap, and the services of a healthy 19-year-old Norwegian *au pair* are all possible answers to the problem of flying with

a two-year-old. So are frontal lobotomies all round. And so is a holiday in Cornwall.

7 Any child old enough to know about Kylie Minogue is old enough to know the name of the country you're visiting and where it is placed on the map. Any child old enough to say 'Please' and 'Thank You' in English can learn two new words to express the same idea. From little acorns . . .

SPAIN

To Spain, with Apologies

Spain is a country hidden, probably more than any other we visit as holidaymakers, from our view. I first went to Spain in 1963. I wasn't fully an adult, but I was certainly not a child. I went to the country without the least idea of its antiquity, let alone its recent history. It was merely a strip of sand lapped by warm water.

There is something balanced and fitting about the relationship between the Spanish and the British holidaymaker. They have sunshine, we have money. A deal has been struck. But when the deal was first proposed, 30 years ago, the negotiators did not meet as equals. Spain was politically isolated and materially poor. Britain by comparison was an international wideboy. 'Give us a bit of your coastline,' we said, 'and we'll bring you big spenders. They can't be separated from their philistine habits, and you'll be obliged to take their sewage as well, but you'll hardly know they're there, trust us.'

There has to be something intrepid about any landing party. Some of the British bridgehead never came home. They opened bars, learned Spanish, and chose to stay on amongst people who were still rooted, with great dignity, in the earth. Ducking and diving was something we had yet to sell them.

I do not mean to say that all that's mean and tawdry on the Spanish Costas is of our doing. The Belgians have not been slouches at leaving their imprint, and given the opening the Spanish have actually rushed to embrace many of our second-rate schemes. But there has been something shameless about the scale of our invasion. Spain was always a land of simple pleasures. The tempo was pedestrian, occasionally hotting up to mule-stroll. And privations, of which there were many, were stoically savoured. Taking the sun on the seafront at Lloret it is easy to forget that Spain is essentially a dark place.

Its churches are dark. Its religion has a strong whiff of Africa. Much of its land is empty and that which isn't gives miserly rewards to those who toil on it. Propriety and honour have held their value. A patrician bearing still looks only slightly old-fashioned. And to be serious-minded is not the embarrassing impediment it can be in Macclesfield. Even the graffiti have a noble gravity about them. *La Pasionaria Vive!* it says on many a wall in Barcelona. Back in Hounslow it is colourfully reported that *Trevor is a Twat*.

I first truly appreciated what separates the Spanish and the British one wintry Sunday on the Costa Blanca. It was late afternoon, and the café where I was loitering with the intent of writing a book was full of Spaniards. Some were dancing in a correct, perpendicular style that was last seen in British dance halls round about 1948. Most were drinking coffee and talking. And since good coffee and good conversation deserve generous allocations of time, they were not in a hurry. There were groups of men. In Britain they might be sitting in the Conservative Club and by four in the afternoon would be royally blotto. If a café could be persuaded to open on a Sunday afternoon in

Britain, men found sitting around its tables in sober and earnest discussion would be considered socially suspect.

There were groups of women too. In Britain, only women with time on their hands meet for coffee, and then on weekday mornings. On Sunday afternoons they knit or garden or wait for the men to come home from the Conservative Club and eat their cremated roast and three veg. They don't sit in public places and linger over a drink.

And then there were the couples, elegant and polite after 30 years of marriage. Here was a difference indeed. The British husband suspects he is married to Flo Capp. The Spanish husband knows he married a goddess. That's why he so often goes elsewhere for sex. It's why on Sunday afternoons he puts on his best suit, brilliantines his hair and offers his arm to Her indoors. He wants to parade her out of doors. He's a very proud man.

Spanish men cannot believe the misfortune of British husbands, whose wives are not fit for pedestals. Sour, graceless women who waddle in ugly cardigans, and sometimes, when the sun shines, wear very little at all. The Spanish can only pity a man condemned to walk behind a slouching harridan and carry her shopping.

The British display a lack of nobility that astonishes the Spanish. Once in Spain I watched an Englishman with time on his hands. His flight home had been delayed. He'd had a couple of beers, been to the lavatory, read a two-day-old *Daily Mirror* from cover to cover, and was seated in uneasy silence next to his wife. Suddenly the airport came to life. A plane had landed. Through a glass screen he and I followed the progress of the incoming tourists, saw them collect their luggage, shuffle through Customs, and emerge hoping to find a porter. That was his cue. 'Gizza job', he cried, and spent the next fifteen minutes carrying suitcases out of the airport to the waiting transit coaches. He made himself useful, and he didn't have to talk to his wife. It was probably the happiest moment of his fortnight on the Costa Dorada, and the *Sindicato Nacional* of Bum Scratchers, Nose Pickers, and Baggage Handlers didn't cry 'Closed shop!' or ask to see his credentials. They just smiled, wondered which mad-house he'd escaped from, and probably talked of nothing else for the rest of the week.

Rolling up your sleeves, clocking on, pitching in, putting in overtime, are not traditional Spanish ways. Taking an extra hour over lunch, taking time to stand and stare – these are. But Spain has a generation, now rising, that wants it all. Microwave ovens, satellite TV, anorexia, three-piece suites, working breakfasts, heart disease. *Mañana* is about to be replaced by the fax machine.

One of the most entertaining spectacles on the Mediterranean shore is the British tourist negotiating the minefield of local food. I am personally acquainted with people who take marmalade to Fuengirola and Rice Krispies to Torremolinos. I have the testimonial of holidaymakers who have notched up 19 years on the Costa Brava and never a brush with garlic, touch wood. And I have journeyed through the lemon groves of Valencia in coaches packed with people who hoped, who fervently hoped, that we'd be able to get a cup of tea.

In tourist Spain it is now easier to find British ale, fish and chips, and a full English breakfast, than it is to find a glass of sherry and a dish of olives. The Spanish are tolerant of this. They recognised long ago that the British need all the help they can get to relax and enjoy themselves. But the bars and cafés created for the British by the British are ugly outposts of the xenophobic tendency. Their handwritten adverts declare clearly what is uppermost in the mind of a Brit when he's holidaying away from home. BEV AND TONY FROM STOKE ON TRENT WELCOME ONE AND ALL. GOOD BEER, ROAST BEEF AND YORKSHIRE PUDDING, CARDS, DOMINOES, AND ENGLISH VIDEOS. Or less politely, HOT AND TIRED? IF YOU ARE, COME ON IN. IF NOT, KEEP BLOODY WALKING!

And there is worse. The nightclubs where the drink is cheap, the hours are long, and the British DJs are proud to promise that you'll see live sex on stage if you just hang around until two punters of the opposite sex have reached the necessary level of drunken degradation. This, in a country where within living memory five-year betrothals were considered hasty affairs, and every courting couple sat in the shadow of a *duenna*.

The number of British people spending their holidays in Spain is falling. Those who can afford to now go to Florida. Spain is left with our pensioners, who remain loyal to her gentle coastal winters and obligingly fill all those empty off-season beds, and she is left with our revolting youth.

I have been embarrassed by the number of Spaniards who have hurried to tell me that *yob* is not necessarily a synonym for *britanicos*. That the Greeks and the Portuguese behave at least

as badly as our boys and sometimes a lot worse. That few Brits get arrested, considering the six million a year who travel to Spain. The Spanish are the most forbearing of hosts.

If some people continue to believe we are the lowest form of animal life along the Costas, it is easy to see why. The worst specimens, our most shameful exports, favour the wearing of the Union Jack. Like our soccer hooligans, they like to have their national colours conspicuously about them – a pair of shorts at the very least – and sometimes, when the evenings grow chilly, they wrap themselves in the great flag itself. So when a troubador band stumbles out of the Talk of the Town Nite Spot, inviting every passing *señorita* to 'Get yer tits out' and vomits spectacularly in the gutter, there can be no question of mistaken national identity. John Bull is alive and none too well in Benidorm.

Within weeks of this book being published someone will write and tell me that they are British, that *they* are regular visitors to Spain, and that none of this applies to them. They travel quietly and independently into the Spanish interior, staying in small inns, eating with the locals, and absolutely never buying a straw donkey. I shall then be obliged to remind them that such behaviour is so rare, many Spaniards don't know it exists. Their eye is drawn anyway by a tidal wave of very different tourists.

The attractions of Spain are easy to identify. First, the sun. Most of the British women arriving in Spanish resorts have a factory pallor. They look grey and tired. Within 48 hours they are red and swollen. Their men acclimatise less painfully. A lot of them work out of doors, so they arrive and leave in pretty much the same condition – deeply tanned and wearing a vest so as to give maximum exposure to their collection of tattoos. A greater acreage of tattooed tributes to *Mam*, and *Denise*, can be seen during the summer season in Spain than anywhere else I have ever travelled.

The second attraction is cheap drink. The amount of alcohol put away for very little outlay is an important index of the success of a holiday. British tourists, like British football thugs, have been raised on hard and urgent drinking. To stay sober is a sign of perversity, to go to bed before the bar closes, a sign of infirmity. To spurn any offer of a free drink is a profligate sin. The British in Spain could be persuaded to spend a day in a rice-grading depot, if they were promised a free bottle of wine at the end of it.

We start drinking when the bars open mid-morning and we keep at it till they close just before the next dawn. The Spanish are no great lovers of early nights themselves. They dine late, and their children eat with them. Still they are amazed at our determination to keep draining glasses long after our brains and tongues have ceased to connect and our children have fretted for their beds.

A third, and important reason that the British enjoy Spain is that there they can experience the ultimate in packaged travel. They can relax, because they know that from the moment they leave Britain to the moment they get back, no hint of foreign-ness need bother them. They can spend a fortnight safe inside a cocoon of Britishness, and if that palls for the more adven-turous, their tour operator can provide them with a quick sanitised foray into the native quarter and back in time for tea. The British in Spain are attached to their hotels by umbilical cords.

When boredom or necessity flushes them out into the cafés and shops of their resort, they are uncomfortable. They know that everyone who makes a living out of tourists has a working vocabulary of at least 30 useful English expressions. Most have a great deal more than that. But there is always the danger that this free linguistic ride will be withdrawn without warning. What if you need the toilet and old Pedro behind the bar pretends he can't understand you? This is the fear that haunts any Brit who ventures beyond the hotel compound.

The obvious solution is to acquire a few words of Spanish. Clearly anyone with the ability to fill in a football pools coupon, or memorise the words of *Viva España*, could learn how to ask for the lavatory or a cup of coffee. On the other hand, why dice with the unknown, and why risk surrendering that reputation for British brass neck? Why not simply shout and mime? And if that fails, why not get very exasperated and say something Anglo-Saxon? This preferred option reinforces the siege mentality. 'We did go out once,' they say, 'but the waitress kept jabbering away, and we couldn't get a proper sandwich, so now we stop in.'

My own level of spoken Spanish is Basic Beginners. The kind of Spanish that gets you dinner and that's about all. Sometimes it gets other people their dinner. Bottle-fed people whose mothers take them to Spain without learning the word for milk. 'Ain't it terrible,' she said, waving an empty bottle at an empty baby, 'when the waiters pretend not to speak English.'

By now the Spanish understand exactly what makes us feel at home. They have got the hang of tea bags and bingo, and they know that the fastest way to make friends with a coach-load of Brits is to tell a joke about a Pakistani, a joke about urinating, and any joke that calls for the accomplished, easy use of a four-letter word. The ice broken, you can then plug them in to a tape of Johann Strauss sambas, and leave them to doze until they are safely back in the hotel.

It is possible that 30 years ago we looked sophisticated. We were different, and we certainly had money to spend. It's understandable that for a while the Spanish were interested in delighting us. Now we have nothing to show them. They are more educated than we are, more politicised, more temperate, more discerning. We are loud but joyless. We are ignorant, petulant, insolent, and crude. Neanderthal mountains of pink flesh, who beat their children and feed them TV dinners. We are the people who brought Mushy Peas to Catalonia.

Imagine, if Paco and Pedro and their mates decided to repay us in kind. Imagine Worthing invaded by men who shout in Catalan. Lulworth Cove full of tapas bars. Imagine Rhyl staying open till midnight. Imagine.

On Being *Giri*

What Not to Do in Spain

Giri is an interesting Spanish word. You don't need to know how to pronounce it because it will never be used *by* you, only *about* you. It describes peculiar foreign habits in general. Essentially, any non-Spanish condition is *giri*. You can do your best, speak the language, adhere to a Spanish timetable, and dress like a regular Madrileño, but you will still be irreformably *giri*. I would like to say that this is why so many Brits make no concessions whatsoever to being amongst the Spanish. I would like to.

Basic *Giri* Explained

1 The wearing of shorts, vests, swimsuits, G-strings, and bare feet away from the beach is very *giri* indeed.

2 The wearing of Union Jacks and large surface areas of lobstered skin are uniquely *giri*.

3 Whatever the temperature, the wearing of anything other than formal dress, hosiery, and footwear is a *giri* giveaway. A fur coat sometimes helps.

4 Sitting at a café table in tight-lipped fury because you've been there 10 minutes and no one has served you, is incredibly *giri*. So is waiting for your turn in a shop. All you need do is politely draw attention to your requirements. 'Oi Pedro!' is rock-bottom *giri*. *'Por Favor'* is fine.

5 To ask for a cup of tea is a *giri* act of foolhardy optimism. You will get a cup of warm milk lightly flavoured with string.

Giri Avoidance for Business Travellers

1 Spain is not so much a country, more an idea. Spanish is something foreigners think they learn at night school. The reality is a collection of powerful regional territories and identities. Castilian Spanish is the second language for many. And to say you are Galician, for instance, is not the Spanish equivalent of saying you're a Yorkshireman. Regional passion should be treated with respect.

2 Adjust your clock. The working day starts at 8.30 am, or no later than 9. It may then go straight through till 3 pm and finish, or adjourn for lunch at 2, resume about 4, and then press on till 7 or 8. Dinner time in Spain coincides with Cocoa Time in Britain, which is why the British often find themselves sitting alone in Spanish restaurants at 8 in the evening.

Except for train departures, timings that are specific to the quarter hour or less – 'I've got a window at 11.20, Thursday. Could we talk then?' – are meaningless. Call it 11.30. Better still, call it sometime between 11 and 12. Don't call it 'around mid-day'. Mid-day can mean 12-ish, but it can also mean lunch time, and as you already know, lunch time is 2 till 4.

3 Words of greeting are important. Prolific thanks are not. This is the opposite of the British tradition whereby you hardly ever say 'Hello, Good Day' to anyone, but say

94

'Thanks' five or six times in the course of buying a box of matches.

4 Spanish surnames look complicated. They are a bit. Instead of bottling out and calling everyone Squire, why not get to grips with their system once and for all? In Spain a man has two surnames, his father's and his mother's, in that order, and so does a single woman. When a woman marries she usually keeps her father's surname and tacks on her husband's patrilineal name. So if Isabella Peralta Perez marries Francisco Garcia Gomez, she becomes Isabella Peralta de Garcia. She might drop the *de*. She might not. And when they have a child he will be Carlos Garcia Peralta.

5 *No* is usually negotiable. The composed, relentless approach works best.

BOWELS

On Going

When the British travel they have something on their mind. Their bowels.

First, will there be anything remotely resembling a British lavatory between here, Positano, and back again? Probably not. But when you think about the average bog back in blighty, is that really so bad? I've run through a fair sample of them in my time, private and public. Doors that don't lock, cracked seats that nip, that sadly absent toilet roll, and the flush that simply won't. My personal awards for the Nation's Worst go to my father-in-law (Domestic Category, Evacuation Likely to Be Interrupted by Landslide of Silver Paper Collected For Guide Dogs), and to Kings Cross BR Station (Public Category, No Flush, No Paper, No Hope, Pay 10p For the Privilege and Vault that Turnstile if You Dare), with a special mention for my mother, (Merit Award for the Cultivation of Constipation, 'Go outside if you're going to make A Smell, and don't pull the chain too hard.')

It is true to say that foreign lavatories sometimes look different from ours, but the basic method of using them is universal. The appliance that vacuums it out of you has not yet been invented. At least, I don't think it has. Maybe I should double-check with all those people in California who offer High Colonic Irrigation.

That possibility apart, we are talking Hole in the Ground. Some have ceramic bowls and warm, user-friendly seats in Pampas Green. Some have foot grips and hand rails. These were invented for people who don't wear knickers. They place the average British tourist, with her polyester slacks, support hose, and commodious drawers, at a disadvantage. Apart from anything else, the hem of her poplin mac may dip into something unsavoury, and where is she going to put her handbag? The earthier versions of this kind of facility are rare these days. Only intrepid travellers are likely to encounter them, and the intrepid already know the score on knickers and handbags . . . and dungarees with straps that dangle . . .

Smart, modern Squat Holes are nearly always optional. The likelihood is that the next cubicle contains something you can recognise as a lavatory. But where there is no choice, all you have to remember is to keep your centre of gravity low, look before you leap, and leap before you flush. Or you could hold on till you get home.

Which brings me to the second lavatorial drawback of travel – Constipation. The British get very tense about irregularity. At home they have attained a kind of balance between fibre, stodge, and mild purgatives. Separate them from that, and they may not go for weeks. I know a woman who takes All-Bran to Austria, and a man who takes Eno's Fruit Salts to the Algarve. Without them they are doomed to dull skin, furred tongue, and shit backing up to chest height. It's no use talking to them about eating vegetables. They are convinced that to look at a lettuce leaf is to invite something a thousand times worse than constipation, something every Brit abroad is waiting to have. The Runs.

Montezuma's Revenge, Delhi Belly, The Cairo Quickstep, The Tegucigalpa Trots. Call it what you like, it's out there waiting for us.

I once saw it suggested that the reason the British succumbed to diarrhoea in such numbers when they're abroad was All That Olive Oil. The theory was that olive oil slipped down the unsuspecting gut and mimicked the well-known effects of liquid paraffin. If that was true 20 years ago, it can't be true now we've taken to olive oil in such a big way. It must be something else. The water, the milk, the fruit, the salads, the ice-cream, the lavatories? A quick look at the recommended precautions makes many people think about cancelling and going to Mablethorpe instead.

Sealed, bottled water only; no ice cubes; no mayonnaise. Beyond that, caution can start to invade the very experience of being somewhere foreign. It's sensible not to risk salads, to peel every piece of fruit, and to refuse all roadside snacks from wayside vendors, fish you haven't recently seen alive, well, and waiting to be eaten, and anything from a cook who never heard of Dettox. Sensible, but depressing. It's too easy, I think, to start seeing a world full of flies with dirty feet and ruthless disease-mongers with faulty microwaves.

Brits often blame their troubles on the local food and overlook the fact that they've overdosed on sun, or alcohol, or both. Then they start knocking back kaolin-based medicines that may help in the short term, or seriously hinder by slowing down the body's natural ability to restore itself. Travellers' Diarrhoea is a self-limiting complaint. If you do nothing but replace lost fluids you'll get better after two days anyway.

Travellers to India used to swear by a mixture of port and

98

brandy as a preventative, and then if that failed, as a cure-all. Nowadays Brits travelling to Calais and all stations east just stick with eating chips. Chips are probably safe, especially if disinfected with Daddies Sauce. If you're brave enough for foreign shopping you can often buy Daddies Sauce abroad, but thousands of British holidaymakers prefer to take theirs with them. But of course even that powerful brew of vinegar, sugar, and spices is no protection against our virulent strain of diarrhoea – the one that exists in the mind.

Free-fall excretion worries the British. At home they are accustomed to rather binding, low residue diets. When they do need to go, which won't be all that often unless Matron happens along with the Syrup of Figs, they are guaranteed privacy. Abroad, where figs grow on trees and dumping is a companionable, open-air activity, they are on permanent alert for the first gripe that will signal farewell to the tightly-closed sphincter, and adieu to the stiff upper lip. Show me a Brit abroad and I will show you a man recently recovered from The Runs, in the very throws of The Runs, or in the late planning stages of his next attack of The Runs. In short, A Case of Diarrhoea Waiting To Happen.

ARABIA

Bridging the Gulf

The Arab world is a very big place. We alight on the North African coast looking for a patch of beach and a spot of haggling in the *souk*, and we are warmly welcomed. Further east, on the Arabian Peninsula, we have played a different role. We have been needed and resented, rewarded and mistrusted, and sun-bathing has not been on the agenda.

Until the 1960s Britain was *the* foreign power in the Arabian Peninsula, and yet we have always dwelt on the periphery of Arab life. We had Political Agents in every territory, and our withdrawal, when it happened, was sudden and based entirely on financial expediency. We were broke.

Philosophically and geographically on the margin, we hopped up and down the Gulf coast with the sole aim of safeguarding our routes to India. We never had any grander territorial ambitions than safe harbours, and we never had any higher hopes than to make life tougher for pirates. Even at the first whisper of oil, our approach was languid. We bought concessions and did nothing with them. Arabia was hot, impenetrable, and full of quarrelsome Arabs, and frankly it didn't seem worth the effort.

Nonetheless, the British itch to organise things wouldn't go away. We got out our pencils and rulers and started drawing territorial boundaries. Our intent was benign, and naive. We really believed we might rewrite thousands of years of nomadic grazing with a line on a map. It suited Arabia to humour us, for the time being.

Suez changed everything. Its aftermath left Britain looking untrustworthy. Militarily, we looked threadbare. And in the face of the nationalism that spread from Egypt across Arabia we were not a daunting enemy. In the places where we had achieved most in the breakdown of tribalism, in the places where we had done the most to democratise, Arab nationalism took its strongest hold. The Arabia we had changed wanted us out. The rest thought it might be nice if we stayed.

The invention of the word *petrodollar* marked the arrival of many Arabs into the 20th century when it was already three-quarters over. The time that followed, when cities were built in the desert and every kind of Brit – honest, opportunist, and fraudulent – was there wearing a safety helmet, *that* was the time when Arabs learned fast and hard about us.

In the late '70s company men swarmed out to the Gulf to make a fast packet. The fact that their enormous salaries, housing, car allowances, and children's school fees were being met through inflated tenders was not lost on the Arabs who were paying the bills. Nor was the fact that expatriates re-turned little to the local economy. The housemaid was likely to be Filipino or Sri Lankan, the shopkeepers were likely to be Indian. And what remained of all that lovely loot was going back to Britain to pay for a small mansion in Surrey. It is an important precept of Arab life that the sharing of good fortune is a sign of true greatness. Grabbing and running is not.

Many of those company men have gone home now. Some

stayed on and are now employed locally. Mainly they are single – a condition held in deep suspicion by Arabs who have little opportunity of sex outside of marriage. They wear their machismo on their sleeve – another cause for mystified concern. (Arab men display their sense of brotherhood by kissing and holding hands, not by punching each other on the chin.) And mostly they are there because they missed the boat home. I never met one who said he was there because he liked it.

Every Arab country is different. Some are overwhelmed by foreign workers, some are still difficult to visit at all. Some have an asceticism that baffles the Western mind, and others are now ruled by minds that have themselves been westernised. Islam is the thread that draws them together, and because we know nothing like it in the West, it is an obstacle to effective discourse between us. At every level, we speak a different language.

Islam takes completely for granted its moral superiority as a social system. Most Muslims who approach the Western fleshpots aren't there because they envy us our habits. They just want to buy a few of our accessories. In so far as our social mores interest them at all, they find us rapacious, short on personal pride, and pathologically hasty.

Anyone who hits a desert airstrip running and plans on being homeward bound three days later, with a deal signed and sealed, is in for a very long, slow shock indeed.

Arabs do buy wristwatches. Apocryphal stories abound in the souks about sheikhs who send out for a dozen Rolexes To Go. They are probably gifts for frenetic British visitors. To an Arab, time is a many spendour'd thing.

Bukra is an Arabic word for *tomorrow*. It is much used, and loosely. There is little practical difference between tomorrow,

102

the day after tomorrow, and next Tuesday fortnight. Except that an appointment for next Tuesday fortnight is not worth the diary page it is written on. 'Tomorrow at 10' is a lightly sketched possibility. If you are expected at that time and arrive later it won't occur to anyone that you are rude, only that circumstances delayed your arrival. You have only to recall how life was lived in Arabia 30 years ago to find this attitude accommodatingly sensible. Making that meeting at 10 wasn't just a matter of jumping on the District Line at Ravenscourt Park and praying for a following wind. In Arabia you arrive if Allah wills it, and one of the most interesting things about the Arab language is that it has no future tense. The imperfect tense covers all ongoing activities, long-term projects and pipe dreams.

The British are pitied for their slavery to the clock. They are seen also as hurrying nowhere in particular. To an Arab, business should be conducted with an open hand and a stately tread. The pleasantries, for which the Arab language has a multitude of set piece enquiries and responses, cannot be skipped. Skating in on a pair of Freeman, Hardy and Willis loafers and saying 'Mike Bishop, Market Development. Perhaps we could start with the Five Year Projections?' will get you nowhere.

Between Arabs a morning meeting will typically begin like this:

'Hello.'

'Hello, and good morning.'

'Good morning. Welcome.'

'Welcome. How is your health?'

'Fine, praise God. How is *your* health?'

'Good, praise God. Welcome.'

'And welcome to you.'

Genuinely solicitous enquiries will be made about your journey, your health, and the well-being of your children. This is not the moment for a self-deprecating joke. Arabs already view us as having a most careless attitude towards our children. 'We've got the little oik down for Borstal' will not amuse. To an Arab, the integrity of his family is more important than any personal achievement, however remarkable. This rule extends to his mother-in-law and any other mature female relations who would be standard joke fodder to a Brit.

We are seen too as being obsessed with secrecy. We make business decisions behind closed doors, and we go to great lengths to conceal our sources and our contacts. We tip someone the wink, he gives someone a nudge, they scratch our backs, and naturally, this being a gentleman's agreement, at some future date we shall scratch theirs. That is not the Arab way.

When a British businessman arrives to do business he's often fazed to find a room full of third parties, not necessarily connected with his mission. Some of them may be the brothers, uncles, and cousins of the Big Man, because in the Arab world nepotism is counted as sound business practice, not as a heinous sin. Others may just happen to be there. They too are having their health and family fortunes enquired after. They too are expected to take coffee. And you, the twitchy Brit in the polyester shirt, are expected to say what you have to say in front of them all. Confidentiality will be respected.

Traditionally, money is something the British hate to discuss. This mystifies Arabs. If you're making a fat profit, why be shy about it? Advertise it with pride! If someone puts some business your way, why whisper down the telephone? Divulge! And pay them the going rate for back-scratching. Above all, never crack jokes about being broke. The British taste for that kind of black humour is not understood by Arabs, nor for that matter by many other people in the world.

Western women who travel on business in Arab countries are assumed to be of very high status and are treated, up to a point, as honorary men. Their numbers are small. The majority of Western women seen by the Arab world are tourists or travelling wives. They are regarded as a kind of third sex and a likely source of trouble and embarrassment. *Fitna* is an Arabic word for an international idea. It means a dangerous female combination of attractiveness and mischief. Expressed in full, in Wakefield or in Wadi Rum, the message is, 'Keep women happy and satisfied, or expect trouble in a seductive guise.' It is a kind of tribute to the scope and power of female influence, even in a society where women are kept on an apparently short rein. Older Arab men will often call out a warning as they approach a group of women. It is a plea to Allah to keep the evil spirits at bay, but is effectively a way of saying 'Pathway, please! Stand clear all women and other instruments of temptation!' It is a line that wouldn't go amiss in a script for *Last of the Summer Wine*.

It doesn't require a lot of imagination to see where this places the blatant sexuality of sunburnt British decolletage. It is to be stared at by anyone with the stomach for it. Lusted after by the expatriate bachelor boys, and hastily covered up by anyone of sensibility. Otherwise we are pitied, if not for our waning importance in the world, then for our lack of manners.

The amount of commercial contact between Westerners and Arab nationals is much diminished these days, especially in the Gulf states. Unless you are a very important Brit, your dealings are more likely to be with a middleman, possibly an Indian or an Iranian. Nevertheless, the basics of Arab etiquette remain important and immutable.

Brit Meets Arab

Twenty-five Useful Rules

1 Before you leave Heathrow, check an Islamic calendar. If it's Ramadan, go home and unpack your case. Businesses do continue to tick over during Ramadan, but the demands and strictures of the season make effective working difficult and it is not the time for taking big decisions or making new friends. At all other times business is barely interrupted by anything. The regular two-day weekend break we enjoy is quite unknown.

2 By way of greeting, women kiss women and men kiss men, usually after shaking hands. Men and women only kiss in private, after marriage. In public, men and women shake hands and so do strangers of the same sex. But you are not a stranger for long in the Arab world and Arab men do kiss Western men once they've grown to know and trust them.

3 Remember the Importance of Being Ahmed. Or Mike. Surnames or family names are only ever used to prevent confusion in a room full of Ahmeds or Mikes. Otherwise there is a jump straight from *Sir – ya ustaaz*, or *Madam – ya sayidah* to first names, in all but the most elevated circles. Titles are generally respected, and the title *Doctor* is deeply revered.

4 Men should never address or smile at a veiled woman. They should treat her as to all intents and purposes invisible.

5 The words Thank You, in response to an offer of something, is interpreted as No Thank You.

6 Three absolute conversational taboos are Sex, Israel, and Pigs.

7 An address should be written entirely in Roman script or entirely in Arabic. This is because the one is a complete reversal of the other – in Arabic the country is written first, and the name last. Addresses in Roman script do get through Arab postal systems, but slowly.

8 Public prayer is widespread and demands absolute respect. Never step on someone's prayer mat. And never video them for the folks back home.

9 For business purposes the Arab world uses the AD calendar. For all other purposes it uses the AH calendar, whose year is shorter by 11 days. That is why Ramadan, in the ninth month of the AH year, falls progressively earlier each AD year. If you need to convert an AH year into AD, use the following formula: $AD = (AH \times 0.97) + 621.54$.

10 The protocol of who goes first through doorways is impossible to pin down. The basic rule is that age precedes beauty, and male precedes female. That rule is often waived for Western guests in general, and Western women in particular.

11 A café in the Arab world is not the same as a café in the West. It is a kind of men's club. For a woman to sit in

one alone is not on, even in a racily Mediterranean city like Alexandria. Two women together might get away with it, but not comfortably.

12 Never admire an Arab's camel saddle, coffee pot, or stainless steel executive toy, because he will feel obliged to offer it to you. Then you'll need to think of something of equal value to give him.

13 If you go bearing gifts, don't expect the wrapping to be born off in a fervour of anticipation, nor to be thanked. You are in Abu Dhabi, not Great Missenden.

14 Overcome the shifty British habit of looking at the floor and picking your nails. Arab men do business looking people in the eye.

15 When in doubt about the propriety of your dress, err in the direction of being completely shrouded. Every travel guide to the Muslim world tells you this, and still Westerners ignore it. Thousands of British visitors wobble through Egypt and Tunisia in short shorts and plunging necklines. Hundreds of them pile down to the camel rides in bikini tops and posing pouches and wonder why they get heatstroke and disrespectful stares. And in places like the Emirates where you can stay inside your hotel and pretend you never left Europe, British wives forget that there are men on the streets who will think the very worst of a woman who flaunts her cleavage.

Generally, if it's long and doesn't cling, you'll be fine and the only sad thing about all this is that it is considered a form of eccentric rudeness for a Western

visitor to wear Arab dress. For Western men, long
trousers and a shirt, with a tie for business, and a tie in
their pocket just in case for social occasions, are
adequate and acceptable. For Western women the
picture is more complicated. Skirts need to be long,
sleeves need to be long and opaque, and necklines need
to be high. Trousers are only acceptable if they are so
voluminous that they don't really look like trousers, and
in Saudi Arabia uncovered hair in any public place is
likely to invite a public telling off from the religious
police.

16 Are your feet clean? Answer, No. You may have washed
them, your socks may be immaculate, and your shoes
impeccable. Nevertheless the soles of your feet are
unclean, because they propel you along the unclean
earth. That's why it's not considered nice to point the
soles of your feet at an Arab. When first told this many
Westerners are perplexed. 'I've never pointed the soles
of my feet at anyone in my life!' they say. 'Why would I
go to Qatar and start?' There are two answers. One is
that if you are entertained in someone's home you are
likely to have to sit cross-legged, on a cushion or a long,
low seat. The second is that men, especially men who are
trying to look cool and confident, often sit with one leg
bent and balanced at right angles to the other. The knee
is way out to the side, occupying plenty of personal
space, the ankle rests lightly on the supporting leg, and
the sole of the foot . . . You got it.

17 And your left hand? Dirty. The left hand was
traditionally used instead of toilet paper and

handkerchieves, and is always used for intimate ritual ablutions before prayer. To eat with your left hand is therefore understandably proscribed amongst Arabs. Several Brits I asked said they found the safest course was to sit on their left hand sooner than forget and give offence.

18 With your left hand out of the way, the taking of coffee seems a less daunting ritual. You take a cup with your right hand and drink it. You accept at least one top-up, and drink it. And when you've had enough you just shake your little cup from side to side and the man with the coffee pot will go away.

19 Returning hospitality is the Brit's Achilles' heel. At home we make noises about a possible return match, safe in the knowledge that we're committing ourselves to nothing. Say 'You must come to dinner some time' to an Arab and he will reply 'When shall I come?' You must then be ready with a genuine proposal.

20 Returning business hospitality isn't easy. You are reduced to using hotels and restaurants and are at an

immediate disadvantage with Arabs who believe home is the place for something so important. Still, there you are in Fujeirah, and clearly it's too far to invite everyone back to Ealing. You do the best you can. Which means making a fuss of your guests. Inviting only their peers. Sparing no effort with the pleasantries. Anticipating their needs. Making it clear at all times that you are in charge. And always offering plenty of food. A Nut and Twiglet Party would be an insult.

21 Never Go Dutch in Arabia. Protestations over who should pay the bill are a polite formality. The host pays for everything.

22 Dieters have a rough time of things at an Arab table. Refusing food is another formality. You only refuse it so that your host may press you harder. Then you give in and eat. You never say 'Just a smidgin of the *tabbouleh* for me, otherwise I shall get my bottom smacked at Weight Watchers.' And where food is served on large communal dishes you never, ever refuse a dish someone else has started on. Do you want to make them look greedy? Do you wish to give the impression that you know something about that dish they don't? Take some! Toy with it as best you can. And keep toying until everyone else seems to be slowing up. If you don't, if you make an ostentatious end to your own eating and announce 'Phew! That's me beaten!', the rest of the table will feel obliged to stop too.

23 You will never be asked to eat sheep's eyeballs. I've been unable to trace the source of this joke, but a joke is precisely what it is.

24 Contrary to legends of old, belching, farting, and picking your nose and eating it carry the same social cachet in the Arab world as they do in Britain. Furthermore, rude jokes are totally unacceptable, even though you are all chaps together. Arabs laugh at banana skins and red noses, not at bodily functions.

25 Alcohol is available to those with the energy to seek it and the cash to pay for it in most Arab countries, and Arabs who like a drink but live in a strictly dry country regularly do a weekend run to Bahrain. Muslims prohibit it because it interferes with the powers of reason. If you normally do business through a malt whisky haze, it would be better to dry out before you leave home than to try and combine withdrawal symptoms with a tricky foreign deal.

FOOD

Fried or Boiled?

From the travelling I did during the writing of this book I have two especially piquant memories of the British seated at foreign tables. One is of a Spanish hotel. It was two minutes' walk from a bakery that opened at eight, and ten minutes' drive from orange groves that were in the throes of a magnificent harvest. But it was a hotel for the British, so its manager was able to serve yesterday's bread and reconstituted orange-style drink, and hold his head high. Far from complaining, his customers were willing to aid and abet him in his mission to serve rubbish and make a fat profit by supplying most of their own staples. Every morning I watched the breakfast ritual of Brits entering a hotel restaurant, their arms laden with jam, crispbread, margarine, and Frosties.

The second memory is of a woman made desperate by the uncompromising purity of Japanese catering. I knew places in Japan where I could get pizza, hamburgers, and *magret de caneton aux cerises*, but that wasn't the point. The Japanese still serve mainly Japanese food, untweaked in deference to any Western palate. It's what I've always said cooks should do. But it is one thing to say it in Britain where the best and worst of all cuisines are available, and another to live by it when you are far from home, hungry, and the dinner on your plate almost certainly just quivered. Shamefully, and briefly, I regretted the Frosties I'd spurned to pack.

At home in Britain, public and domestic styles of eating only converge in a very few middle-class foodie families. For the rest, food eaten Out is fancy, food eaten In, plain. The two experiences have only this in common – no matter how bad, we will not complain. This is both a measure of the importance of food in our lives, and of our unease with complaining in general. Food is something we stoke up on. We shop for it grimly, list in hand, and rarely surrender to seasonal surprises. The more we earn, the more we spend on everything but food, and it is a common fact of British family life that food is bolted, plates are cleared, and the slowest eater is left to finish alone.

So many foreign cooks have been able to graft their style onto British eating that it's hard to say what ever was traditional British food. Our attitudes to eating are easier to identify. The constant tension between pleasure and necessity. The squeamishness and fear concerning the provenance of bits of animals and unknown fruits. The preference for something bland gussied up with one of Heinz's 57 varieties. The pot of well-stewed tea as the fulcrum of every meal. The haste. The stoicism.

We travel most comfortably to the United States, the only other country in the world where the idea of a Chicken Tikka Pizza does not jar, and though there may not be any tannin-lined tea pots, there are certainly tea bags and hot water. America's state-of-the-art international-concrete-mixer approach to food is what you get when you take the British method and add lots and lots of money. The only problem hungry Brits have in the land where you can have extra

115

chopped nuts on *anything*, is what to choose. When we travel to other places, it's a different story.

The British stomach operates on Nordic Meal Time. It likes something for breakfast, something at noon, and then at least two other sessions at the trough before bedtime. These can be high tea, and a late supper, or afternoon tea, followed by dinner, or even tea, dinner, and a thick, milky nightcap with the calorific value of a steamed treacle sponge. Our stoking patterns are so idiosyncratic to each family that when the British invite you round for the evening it's a serious worry whether you should expect a four-course dinner or a cup of Ovaltine.

In Germany and the Netherlands, where it is easy to wrap yourself round the outside of a cream cake any hour of the day, the British can relax. Place them in a Mediterranean context and you will find them at three in the afternoon, looking balefully at shuttered *patisseries* and wondering how they can possibly last till dinner. They should have eaten more at lunch, taken 40 winks, and paced themselves for the long haul, but the habit of a flabby sandwich and a quick half of mild is very hard to break.

There are travelling Brits, smitten by the sun on the water, who are wholly in favour of anything foreign, even if it is grilled training shoe insole served with chips and a load of lip from the *patron*. But there are thousands more for whom the word *meal* signifies something hot, with potatoes and peas, all held in place with a gel of Firm Control Bisto. It isn't surprising. This is the food we were raised on.

Toying with a dish of perfect black olives, anticipating the fragrant *estouffade* that will not disappoint, yearning for another piece of bread, and ending it all in an intimate encounter with a freshly plucked fig – these are experiences that do not translate well into English. They keep you at the table far too long. The British like sex and food to be over with as quickly as possible so that they can get cleared up and listen to the Shipping Forecast.

The foreplay of little palate ticklers is rather lost on the British. They've always been in favour rather of getting stuck straight in to the meat and potatoes, though they've conceded that soup has its place, but only if it is brown or red. If there's one thing that will throw a hungry male Brit off his stride it is green soup. 'Why is it green?' he wonders. And 'Is it medicinal?' Brown soup is much safer. Best of all is red. Tinned tomato soup is the fastest way to quell his fears that he may be asked to eat something Fancy. British women are sophisticates by comparison. They have abandoned the nation's favourite indelibly staining soup and taken to prawn cocktail in a very big way.

While the rest of Europe lingers over crudités, the British forge ahead. In Spain and Italy I have seen tables turned round by British parties at three times the speed of other nationalities. In a restaurant, the two things uppermost in a Brit's mind are a) where are the lavatories? and b) can we get just a snack? And when it becomes clear that a meal must be ordered, what he would most like is everything on one plate and no funny sauces. Separately served vegetables can add hours to a meal, and sauce should be a matter for a man's own taste and conscience. When a Brit orders *poulet forestière*, clearly it's a bit of chicken he's after. And if orders hake, hake is what he wants, with peas and potatoes. And if that hake has come into unfortunate contact with a *sauce rémoulade* then somebody really ought to scrape it all off.

The British are very firm about sauces. Let foreigners fret about undercooked *roux* and cloudy *bouillon*. Has no one told

them you can get sauce in a bottle? You can get it in red or brown, and there's a special yellow one invented to make the eating of lettuce a meaningful experience. And if your dinner is still insipid, there are malt vinegar, English mustard, and Worcester sauce, all sold in bottles, but regrettably not always available in foreign parts. Prudently, many travellers now take their own. Armed with his sauce bottle, the Brit knows he has a better chance of piecing together A Proper Dinner.

A Proper Dinner should contain meat. It can contain fish but only if all traces of skin, bone, fins, eyes and other wobbly bits have been removed. Crustaceans, shellfish and all other creatures that are wobbly *per se* are just not on. Meat is an altogether safer bet. For preference it should come from a cow, a pig, a sheep or a fowl no smaller than a rugby football. Apart from dangerously inbred aristocracy, the British do not eat small birds on toast. Nor do they willingly eat horse, dog, rabbit, or most categories of innards.

Organs that once pulsed and appendages that once dangled do not make the British mouth water. We need our meat to look as little as possible as though it once helped propel an animal across a farmyard. The few Brits who eat tripe will only

118

buy it when its appearance has been so sanitised that it is unrecognisable to foreign tripe freaks. It is as though we were too rudely and abruptly snatched from country life, our rural dream too cruelly shattered by factory chimneys, to be able to think of animals now without dressing them in jackets and mittens. When a Brit says he wants meat he doesn't mean brains, or tongues, or a bowl of sheep's feet soup. He means a chop, or a steak. And he wants it with peas and potato.

The attachment of the British to the potato is a remarkable thing. They are an indispensible element in every meal, even when that meal contains rice or pasta. This is because we are a bit hazy about nutritional balance, and anyway we like spuds. We hold them in such high esteem that we have perfected *two* different ways of cooking them. You can have them fried. Or you can have them boiled. The French, who understand nothing of the potato, steam them, sauté them, slice them thinly and bake them in cream, and frequently leave them out of meals altogether. They have to, to make room for courgettes and stuff like that.

The British do eat other vegetables. I don't mean to suggest that we never do things with carrots and cabbage. Indeed some of our achievements with vegetables have earned us a place in the Guinness Book of Domestic Crimes. Our forte is the Long Slow Boil. British cooks learned long ago that this technique is doubly useful for subduing signs of life in all *brassicas* and recreating the smell of a flatulent skunk. Similarly with root vegetables. We are drawn to the least attractive specimens, the grotesquely twisted, the mutantly huge, and we boil them until we have put them out of their misery. So when we travel we are unnerved by the sight of small turnips that look good enough to eat. We panic, and demand that other touchstone of A Proper Dinner – peas. Not fresh, not served in the pod, but tinned will be fine, and frozen would be perfect. Just a spoonful. A small British gesture to the vegetable kingdom.

Sometimes it's a question of salads. To the world at large salads are little confections of leaves and herbs, to be picked at and savoured. To the British a salad is a meal, but not A Proper Dinner. It should contain lettuce, cucumber, and tomato, egg boiled until the yolk has turned grey, and a nice big slice of pink plastic pork product. But the key to authenticity is in the garnish – a *macédoine* of pickled beetroot and a dollop of salad cream that will bleed into each other and create an interesting shade of yuck. When the British are served salads abroad, they don't see them as restoratives or whetters of the appetite. They can only wonder at people who serve lettuce with another sort of lettuce, and ask themselves 'Where is the beetroot?'

If a Brit cannot have his beetroot, then at least let him have pudding. There may be weaknesses in our national cuisine, a lack of pride in regional specialities, a passive receptivity to the odds and ends of all immigrant styles, but on puddings we are immovable. We like Instant Whip, and any combination of suet, apples, and custard. And if we're eating out, if our expectation is of something fancy, the thing we long to see on the Sweet Trolley is a freshly-thawed Black Forest Gâteau. In the Persian Gulf, in a hotel much used by Brits, I was nearing the end of an Arab meal – billed as a Novelty Event – and had belly-danced my way to the dessert buffet. There, amongst the *baklava* and the *konafa*, the pistachios, the dates, the apricots, and the rosewater, was a grotesque presence, a sight with the same surreal force as a camel riding in the back of a Toyota pick-up – an unbreached BFG. It was, the manager assured me, *de rigueur*.

The British may not have known this caterer's travesty for long, but they are now fiercely devoted to it. It has confirmed their preference for puddings that have been *made*, as distinct to things like peaches and grapes that owe their existence to God and photosynthesis. In tourist Spain, where the British have had plenty of time to educate the locals in the essentials of good cooking, for some reason, native stubbornness perhaps, you still can't get a rhubarb crumble. But do they give in and eat melon? They do not. They choose something else that bears the interfering mark of mankind, something else he's managed to synthesise out of hydrogenated vegetable fat, partially inverted refiner's syrup, whey powder, sodium alginate, and a purple liquid that doesn't cause cancer – a dish of Ice-creams Various.

And something to drink? Not necessarily. The British are often happy to go right through a meal on the promise of a cup of tea at the end of it. Never great drinkers of wine or water, they prefer to take their beer standing in smoke-filled bars, and a view I've often encountered amongst British mothers is that drinking at table is not a habit to encourage because it fills you up before you've had your pudding. Gravy and custard should be liquid enough. If they're not, and in many British families the specific gravity of the gravy is an index of the cook's excellence, then that cup of tea will be all the more worth waiting for.

We've never really got the hang of coffee. We now buy record quantities of instant coffee granules, but countries with a long history of coffee-drinking don't count that. The British are waiting for someone to invent a foolproof method of making coffee. But no one is going to do it because no one else finds it difficult. In this and other respects there is something childlike about the British at table.

We don't like difficult food, complicated food, food that has to be wheedled out of its shell, green food, raw food, or food that may give us zest or lascivious desires. Garlic worries us, mushrooms terrify us, and olive oil gives us the runs. We like Mother's Pride, pickled onions, and evaporated milk. We search foreign village stores for Shredded Wheat. And when we camp in Provence we hope and pray we've packed enough Angel Delight. The United States is one of the few destinations we can make for and know that alongside the jalapeño peppers, and the kasseri, and the muffins that are cakes, and the jello that is jelly and the jelly that is jam, we shall find meat and potatoes in some recognisable guise and we shan't go to bed hungry. Out for the count perhaps, like a python that's snacked on a small antelope, but definitely not hungry.

USA

Poor Relations and Special Friends

A few years ago, when I first announced I might be going to the United States, people hurried to tell me that I was sure to be treated handsomely over there because of my endemic British cuteness. Inflamed by this attractive prospect, I got my visa and went. It turned out my well-wishers had been wrong. The Cutie Factor was a spent force, the free ride on re-runs of *Upstairs Downstairs* was over. Outside of Nebraska the *cachet* of being British was no longer worth much at all.

The United States of America takes itself very seriously. Self-deprecation, which is a national sport to the British, has never caught on there. Woody Allen's success at marketing such flaky behaviour is one of the great unsolved riddles of our time. As a starting point in the exploration of the mid-Atlantic abyss this is very useful. After all, if we are looking at Life, Destiny, And All That from the opposite ends of the telescope, the fact that we kind of share a language isn't going to help.

The mythology of Cuteness was rooted in the unease Americans feel when they're with real foreigners. Of course, America is full of foreigners. I've met more Afghanis in the United States than I've met Sioux Indians. But these are the sort of foreigners who arrive with one small parcel, enter the Dream Machine, and emerge soon after with track lighting, a shrink, and an easy payment plan with a funeral home. Assimilated foreigners. The real ones, who don't speak a word of Hollywood English and refuse to see the point of air-conditioning, disturb Americans. They feel glad about the enormous oceanic moat they've got either side of them. So if they had to be cosmopolitan at all, they were relieved to have the diluted experience of meeting the British.

Most Americans understand one another. In the South they drawl, in the Bronx they nasalise, and in Washington they do funny things with their vowels, but across the land man can speak to man without thinking 'I'm going to need an interpreter' or 'Gosh! Not quite One Of Us I fear!' In comparison, Britain has a kaleidoscope of socially significant accents. Half an hour on a London Tube, east to west, takes you through two fiercely defended linguistic territories. Lancastrians whisper in Yorkshire pubs. I am related by marriage to Scots who may as well speak Berber for all I understand of them. Coping with all this used to make the Americans feel good. Here were foreigners who at least tried to speak American.

That was the honeymoon. Now so many British go to the United States, it is over. We fail to charm them. We don't even try. It's a relationship between a precocious child and a testy old-timer, delightful for five minutes and then a strain. We British have seen it all, done it all, had it all worked out before the USA was even invented. National exuberance and self-confidence bores us. People who try so hard embarrass us because well, let's face it, making an effort just isn't cool. We didn't get where we are today by Going For It.

One of the most profound culture shocks of my life occurred at dinner with Americans I had never met before. 'I'm

Seymour and this is Rhoda. We're from Bayside, New York, gotta car valeting business, a condo on Key West, and three grandchildren. How 'bout you folks?' I am no shrinking violet. My partner is the kind of man who chats to supermarket checkers. We began to mumble. We fiddled with our iced water, rolled up the hem of the tablecloth and managed to stutter that he was in wine in a small way, and I was a bit of a writer. Did we have any children? 'Yup.' Were they as good-looking as us? 'Nope.' Blood from a stone would have been easier.

I spent that whole evening wrong-footed. Blinded by Seymour's bridgework? Stunned by the reflection off Rhoda's portable Gold Reserve? Only slightly. Mainly I was winded by all that assured self-projection. Seymour and Rhoda had clearly never entertained a moment of self-doubt in their combined one hundred and seven years in Bayside and Key West, and the United States is populated with Seymours and Rhodas. Their view of the world is that if you rise early, work hard, and fight clean, everything will be fine, and if it isn't you can trade it in and get a better deal. Sagging jowls and showers that aren't the perfect temperature can be fixed, so can communists; and the latest thing is, even death may be optional.

This is not the British way. We know that things are always worse than they seem, you can't beat the system, things never get better if you pick at them, making a fuss never got anyone anywhere, and pigeon shit always has someone's number on it. Life is a heavy bummer, and philosophically we are on a collision course with Americans. Nothing illustrates this better than the way we shop.

At home, we are the world's most docile shoppers. We don't haggle, we are forbidden to handle the merchandise, we queue, we allow ourselves to be chivvied, and we always preface our requests with an apology. We take all this with us when we go to America, and are unsettled by the discovery that in the United States, sales staff hope and expect to sell. Unlike their British counterparts who are reluctant to let anything but shop-soiled junk leave the store, American sales staff expect you to know what you want and not to rest till you get it.

In the United States it is not considered rude to start by saying 'Gimme a can of that stuff for soft lenses' or 'I'll take three of these couches and I'll ship them.' In the United States only nut-cases and Brits start by saying 'I don't suppose you'd have this in my size?' We stand at delicatessen counters and say 'Er . . . a sandwich? Any tuna?' *Any tuna!* Of course any tuna. Also, what kind of bread do you want, what kind of lettuce, capers, onion, soft cheese? Do you want it big? Do you want it huge? And tell us please because we're dying to know, do you want it with mayo?'

We take our supine shopping habits into clothes departments, and even though we don't have three legs and a hump we are sceptical about finding anything that fits. They feel sorry for us. We find it remarkable that electrical goods are sold with plugs fitted, but we're quick to note that there's sure to be a catch in it, like a higher price tag or a conspiracy to electrocute everyone who buys Ring-O-Let Curling Tongs. They think we're crazy. Worst of all, we order ice-cream and don't even known if we want extra chopped nuts. Untravelled Americans could be forgiven for thinking that Brits shop at Gum and get publicly flogged for doing it.

Not only are we uncomfortable about our wants and appetites, we are even more uncomfortable about being able to afford them. Our '80s Yuppies who brayed about their latest mega-kill on the futures market were a national aberration. The correct British approach to money is to pretend you don't

have any, and if the evidence against you becomes unmanage-able, at least demonstrate how frugal you are with it. In the United States, if you buy yourself one of those lawn-mowing buggies, you invite everyone round to admire it and you tell them what it cost. In Britain you pretend you got it at a car boot sale.

When we are at home to American visitors, this trait still scores modestly on the Cuteness Register. As tourist attrac-tions, palaces with worn carpets and pubs liveried in nicotine and sputum do earn their keep. But to willingly live like that? They know we love our Queen because it says so in the papers. What they don't understand is why. They think it may be about *noblesse oblige*, and the Blitz, whereas she has actually earned all that affection by never throwing away a pair of old curtains. The Americans, who can see *exactly* where the Duchess of York is coming from, and who would love to get the Chancellor a new Budget bag, think this is all a clever publicity stunt. But it isn't. It's a congenital British condition.

When we take it across the Atlantic, it looks shabby. At Government level, if it's very good quality shabbiness and displayed with enough self-possession, it gets by. This is one of the few things to be said for spending your childhood at Eton. The rest of us look down-at-heel, and we know it the moment we arrive. We're also slightly put out by hotels that aim to excel.

I still find myself behaving like a child in a toy shop the first hour I'm in an American hotel room. Proper mixer taps! An ice machine! And then, when I get home, I join all those other world-weary Brits in that chestnut of dinner party talk, The Demise of the Proper Hotel. 'Of course' someone opines, just back from the Kansas City Marriott, 'the Americans have sanitised hotel life out of sight.' 'Wherever you go in the world', chips in his friend, lately liberated from the Seattle Sheraton, 'the Americans have homogenized the travel experience. A Holiday Inn is a Holiday Inn. Burgess Hill, Burkina Fasso, what's the difference?' 'Wouldn't it be wonderful', enthuses the man who has to stay at the Hyatt Regency because it's a corporate reservation, 'to find one of those sweaty old places, down on the main square, with a ceiling fan, and scorpions in the beds, and a man in a greasy vest who spits tobacco on the floor when you ask about food . . .' And everyone agrees that it would be simply marvellous.

Slumming for chic is another thing Brits do that baffles Americans. Why go to the South Bronx with your heart in your mouth when you can see it in films? Why brave Castro and Mission in search of Real People when there are Real People in Sausalito? It's back again to differing senses of our place in the scheme of things. Americans know that if they invest enough energy and money they can have smarter kids, a faster car, and an option of life everlasting, preferably in Florida. Brits know that the higher you climb the further you fall, skid row is just around the corner, and owning a Regency table does not guarantee anything except that someone will scratch it for you.

This is the source of British humour, and America doesn't get it.

In the United States there's nothing funny about a lot of things. Alcohol is one of them. Somehow we forget that Britain is one of the very few places in the world where public drunkenness isn't a matter of shame. In the States, boozy lunches don't happen. Business drinking is modest and disciplined. And Americans may brag about the size of their freeways and their refrigerators, but they never brag about the size of their hangovers. That would diminish their self-esteem, which is enormous, and it would offend their idea of moral rectitude.

Like the British, Americans don't really care for sex, but their tactics for dealing with it are different. Americans analyse it earnestly, search for new erogenous zones, and then go shopping. Brits joke about it. When they travel to America they should leave their jokes behind, because British women, the carbolic-scented sirens and termagants who are the butt of all those stories, are nothing like the Daughters of America. Clearly, British women are powerful, but it's the kind of power achieved by silently tunnelling beneath the foundations. Americans, who prefer to talk their way in and out of trouble, find this peculiar.

They cover all personal data and basic psychological glitches with disarming frankness in the first hours of a relationship. I've been trusted with the birth signs, back problems, and sibling resentments of Americans faster than I've learned the names or professions of fellow British party guests. Not surprisingly they find our social reticence chilly, and our marital silences sinister. I believe one of the most useful preparations a Brit can make for a trip to America is to become enthusiastic about something, preferably himself, and practise talking about it without recourse to words like *slightly*. Then, if time permits, he might run through his trustiest personal anecdotes and expunge all irony. It's not a question of caving in to the Yanks. Just the courtesy of trying to make yourself understood.

Finally, after we've learned to speak up and pay up, two more minefields lie waiting to blow up in the face of that Special Relationship. Christianity. And Patriotism. Fundamentalism is on the rampage everywhere in the world, and nowhere less so than the United States. It's too easy for British visitors, of no religious persuasion in particular, to underestimate its importance.

We still have a mainly relaxed relationship with God, claiming membership of one of His clubs when we want a church wedding or we think we might be about to die, and telling gentle jokes against Him the rest of the time. My own inclination for spiritual shopping around has prompted strangers to write and tell me they pray for my mortal soul, but in Britain no one has ever thumped me for it. In America my benign Godlessness has lost me several friends. So has my scepticism about the Americans, or the British, or the Dinkas of Sudan being God's Own.

Allegiance to the flag is a serious matter. Flag-waving in Britain is confined to small children waiting to greet Royalty, and Neo-Nazis with Special Learning Difficulties. People who fly the Union Jack from a flag-pole at the bottom of their garden are assumed to be harmlessly dotty, and Union Jack boxer shorts are not considered disrespectful. In the United States people stand for the Stars and Stripes. They put their hands on their hearts. Tears fill their eyes. They really mean it, and they can only pity a people that uses its national symbol for wiping the dishes.

It is safe to say America does not look up to us. We used to be able to pull rank with our antiquity, but these days you can get some terrific fakes. And how can you look up to people who so love being *down*? We are mumbling, stumbling bundles of diffidence. We think small, eat like sparrows, and our luggage doesn't even match. Cute, as you can see, no longer counts.

Coast to Coast

When the British talk about America they mean New York and California. Mainly they mean New York, and in ten years' time they will also mean Orlando. My own experience of America is only of New York and San Francisco, two of the most extraordinary cities in the world and neither of them typically anything. The contrasts between those two particular bits of America-on-Sea are startling. British businessmen who have got the East Coast worked out have to start all over again when they go West, and knowing a little of the language does nothing to dilute the fact that America is big and foreign.

San Francisco

San Francisco – and incidentally, only middle-aged hippies from Tufnell Park call it Frisco – San Francisco has nothing to do with Europe. It faces the Orient, it thinks Orient, and much of its population neither knows nor cares where Europe is. If you are white and heterosexual and you are planning a trip to San Francisco, it is worth remembering that while you are there you will belong to a kind of ethnic minority. The language most spoken there is Chinese. The sexual climate is a highly politicised brand of homosexuality. It is also one of the easiest places on earth to be a straight, white visitor.

San Franciscans are forgivably smug about their sunshine and scenery and cannot understand why one of the first questions the British ask is 'When's the next earthquake?' My favourite Californian joke explains their position. 'Why did God give Washington all the lawyers, New York all the bankers and San Francisco the San Andreas Fault? San Fran-

132

cisco had first choice.' In Japan, hotel guests are issued with earthquake advice the moment they check in, and earthquake drills are a regular part of working life. In San Francisco you can go to a special cinema and experience what an earthquake *feels* like, but no one will hound you with lists of what to do if it really happens. If you asked the answer might be, 'Sip your wine, take a last look across the Bay, and remined yourself no one's immortal.'

The city has a reputation for sinfulness. Also for convention breaking, the wearing of loudly coloured shirts, and all kinds of flaky behaviour from men with pony tails. In fact it is Dinky Town. Dual Income, No Kids. The Dinks have lots to spend, and in San Francisco you can shop till you drop. It is a city that is frankly rich but spiritually very Zen, and if those two make strange bedfellows, when the British climb between the sheets the effect is even stranger. In general Brits are ill at ease with gloss and money. A perfect cup of coffee served in perfect surroundings by a smiling and eager waiter makes a Brit happy but deeply suspicious. Why doesn't someone snarl, 'Meals only.' Why isn't there a crack in the saucer or a hair in the sugar? And what is the price tag on all that smiling?

The price tag is that you have to act the same way. If you try to be British in San Francisco you'll look as though you've been cryogenically preserved. Silent, glum, worried someone might invite you home. The energy and style of the world British businessmen encounter makes their domestic scene look slow and shackled. In California the day starts early and everything is tackled with joyful vim. Businesses start early because of time zones. When it's 7 am in San Francisco, Wall Street is open in New York. Working breakfasts have replaced the working lunch, and in hotel dining rooms I have seen strong men do two breakfasts back to back.

Lunch, in a city where it's difficult not to spend all your time putting wonderful things in your mouth, is brief, or missed. The mid-afternoon haze of Armagnac that still precedes a British board of directors as they stagger back to the desk is unknown, and in California, where the very latest in physiology is always hot news, they avoid serious lunching because it causes Concentration Dip.

Dinner is different. San Franciscans dine, but rarely for business. They do it for pleasure, they don't keep late hours, and they are just as likely to invite you to their place as to a restaurant. The point of inviting you home is to give you an amazingly good time, feed you, get to know you, and probably to introduce you to lots of people they think you'll like. They don't really want to talk business – though they may interrupt dinner to take business phone calls and think nothing of it – but they will if you insist. What they want is to thaw the British chill. The three stages of At Home business entertaining that all British couples run through as a matter of routine – 1) Avoidance, 2) Reluctant Issue of Invitation, and 3) blind panic, dread, and obsessive counting of unchipped wine glasses upon acceptance – are rare in California.

Snapshots of your children and your dogs are one of the most

useful accessories you can have with you. Tins of shortbread with pictures of Loch Lomond are very nice to give, but little insights into your life back in Britain are valued much more. They ease the uphill work of persuading a Brit to unclench his gluteals and talk about himself.

Finally, and coincidentally connected with uphill work and gluteals, the thing I most wished I'd been warned about in San Francisco. When you're on foot and heading for an appointment in a place you've never been before, a map of the city is of limited value. It will show you how many blocks you have to go. But it may conceal the important fact that you are in for a vertical climb. In the event of cable cars not passing that way, you will need sturdy shoes, crampons, and twice as much time as you first thought.

New York

New York has always appealed to the British. We know London is bad and we enjoy the idea of somewhere that's worse. The first qustion asked of a Brit when he says he's just back from New York is, 'Was it terrible?', and when he replies, 'Saw two murders, three muggings, and a suicide', everyone feels deeply gratified. There's nothing the masochist in us enjoys so much as a good shudder.

When Americans come to London we know they'll want to do Big Ben, some royal bits, and the shops in Regent Street. For a racier itinerary we might include Carnaby Street. But we don't expect them to enquire about trips to Tower Hamlets. When the British go to New York their attitude is different. They are no sooner there than they start wondering about Harlem and the Bronx. They weigh up their chances of being able to get to Yankee Stadium and back in one piece, and fantasise about dining out on the anecdotes when they get back to Waltham Cross.

The apogee of intrepid travel for the Brit in New York is to use the Subway. It is filthy, noisy, and cheap, and so is better than the London Underground on one count, but its reputation is awful. The word is, it can be fatally dangerous. In fact very few people die there, and certainly not many more than die on the Paris Metro or the London Underground. Lots of people get robbed, especially on the night trains, but the greatest danger is from something else. Getting Lost.

In the Subway all maps, signs, and direction boards have been assiduously covered with graffiti. So have the train windows, so there's no point in peering out tentatively to see where you are. You need to *know* where you are. You need to know the name of the line, whether it goes by any other fancy names – such as the Seventh Avenue Local, which turns out to be the same thing as the West Side I R T – and how to get out of the station once you've arrived. Otherwise you do risk death. From starvation and exhaustion. Native New Yorkers tend to know one journey by heart. They know the only route-planner they can rely on is the one inside their head, and the safest and fastest way to put a Subway notch on your belt is to tag along with a veteran and hold onto his sleeve.

Taxis are easier. There are only three essentials for a successful cab ride in New York. Some knowledge of Spanish. The ability to re-hang a car door. And a very clear idea of how to get to your destination. On a bad day, when the Queens–Midtown Tunnel is at a standstill and the Williamsburg Bridge looks grim, your friendly New York cabbie will turn and ask you for suggestions. Very often the best suggestion you can make is that you should settle your account, get out, and walk.

To walk a north–south block takes me two minutes, and

nearer five when it's rush hour and I'm wearing high heels. To walk an east–west block takes two to three times as long. What you always need to know is the name of the junction nearest your destination. Just *Madison Avenue* isn't a lot of help. You could have a five mile walk. You could arrive very late. Or in a body bag.

New York is changing. There's less money about, and less energy. There are still ruthless people who will kill you for your table reservation at the *Quilted Giraffe*, and single women who'd do anything for a date with a man who isn't a psychopath or someone's husband. But New York is easing up. Corporations are moving out from Manhattan. Couples who scrabbled to get themselves a loft in Tribeca are beginning to wonder why. And on Friday afternoons all those men in grey suits try to escape to the country. To spend a summer weekend in the city is an admission of social failure.

Relaxation in New York is very tiring. You can run, speed-walk, do weights, see your therapist, count the coins in your piggy bank to see if you have enough yet for theatre tickets, or read the latest How To book. In Britain there is something embarrassing about being seen buying *Close That Deal*. You want the shop assistant to put it inside a paper bag fast. In New York everyone will be reading it, talking about it, and doing the test exercises in broad daylight. They know that if they don't keep up they'll be out, desk cleared, name unscrewed from the door, and home for an early shower.

New York executives live in a permanent state of red alert. There is no coasting or fudging and no hesitation in telling a man that he'd be happier elsewhere. The perch everyone is after is Chief Executive. To become a President is to lower your expectations. Vice-President is only a few steps short of the scrap heap. The shambolic British style of management, with fumbling presentations and poor old Stan being kept on because he's been with the company 30 years and his wife's got nerves, is not known in New York. There, Stan would have been escorted from the building 29 years ago.

British businessmen often wonder what to do with their evenings in New York. Strolling isn't always advisable. Singles bars are bad news. The answer is to have an early night. Stay in, shine your shoes, trim those troublesome nostril hairs, practise walking confidently towards your mirror and saying 'I'm Stan Barraclough. How are *you* today? I'm Stan Barraclough. How *are* you today?' And then hit the sack with a copy of *Close That Deal*. In a plain brown wrapper of course.

Ten Short Walks to the Heart of America

1 Don't expect signs that say *Toilet* or *Lavatory*. Think euphemism. Think *Rest Room*, or *Comfort Station*.

2 If someone tells you what grade their kid is in, add a six. This will give you the child's age, approximately.

3 In a restaurant, 'Please wait to be seated' is the Eleventh Commandment. Your table captain shows you to your table, and a bus boy does the rest. Both will introduce themselves, which is handy because you can then call, 'Oh Sheldon!' when you want more bread. Both will probably enquire 'How are you folks?' The answer is 'Fine'.

4 In the USA food is eaten mainly with forks or fingers. Knives are for killing people. Or for cutting up their man-sized steaks into fork-sized pieces.

5 The complexities of eating fried eggs are an indicator of how easy it is to succumb to Menu Burnout. Sunny side up means the egg hasn't been flipped over. Easy Over, Over, and Over Hard are eggs fried on both sides and with yolks in diminishing states of runniness.

6 Tea comes iced, creamed or with lemon, but never with boiling water and cold milk. Regular coffee is black. Sometimes it isn't.

7 Never run away from a policeman. He'll shoot you.

8 American beaches are places where you keep your clothes on and play volleyball. There is no topless jiggery-pokery, and no wrestling with your bathing trunks under a towel.

9 God and the Book of Genesis are Very, Very Big in America.

10 In spite of this, try not to die there. There is no such thing as a cheap and simple send-off.

JUST JOKING

North Americans are some of the most serious and literal-minded people in the world. There are many of life's slings and arrows that they do not see as raw material for humour. Only as problems waiting to be solved. What's more, they don't even have any neighbours to joke about. They see Canadians as disadvantaged cousins, and Mexicans as picturesque characters in a holiday theme park. Basically, the United States are too sure of themselves for nervous laughter.

On the other hand, the French joke about Belgians, the Swedes about Norwegians, and the Danes about Finns. Tell the world which of your neighbours you like to laugh at, and the world will immediately know who you are and what primitive inferiority complexes keep you awake at night. When neighbouring countries don't joke about each other it is only because both have unshakeable confidence in their innate superiority. The famine of French jokes about the British and British jokes about the French is no mere accident of language or wit.

Actually, the French and the British do laugh at each other. The French enjoy the occasional chortle about our class warfare, and the British are amused by the idea of expertise between the sheets. But that's all. The French are so free of doubt about their superiority to the British that they have no need of jokes. And we don't waste ammunition on the patently odd and inferior French. Race-baiting in Britain is a mainly domestic affair.

We joke about the Irish, because we feel we must have someone to stand between us and permanent custody of the Thick Man of Europe Award. We joke about Asian shopkeepers out of idle envy. And we joke about West Indians because we fear they really may possess irresistible sexual magnetism. We denigrate in our immigrants the qualities we'd most like to see in ourselves. But when we want a really good laugh we look no further than the mirror.

The British are famous for their self-deprecation, but not unique. The Italians are very good at it too, though when you look closer in Italy it really amounts to regional warfare, Tuscan against Roman, everyone against Sicilian, and so is only a variation on that commonplace need to prove that your neighbours are dim. When the British knock themselves, they do it at a personal level, and pull no punches. This is admired, as a sign of enormous national self-confidence, but only by the British themselves. To others, who wall themselves in with concepts like pride and dignity, the British sense of humour is perverse.

In two fields of humour we have achieved world domination. Class, and Women. Other nations have class systems, and some of them are cruelly rigid. The British system is a rich source of laughs because it's so open and mobile. It isn't what people *are* that amuses us, so much as what people aspire to. Social clambering is one of Britain's most popular sports. It's tough to do and fun to watch, and the rest of the world is

genuinely bewildered by the chuckles we get out of what people hang inside their cars, and the names they give their children. And Brits don't just laugh at the hardware of snobbery – the garden gnomes and the EPNS cutlery, the muesli, the carphone, and the butler kept in mothballs in the East Wing. They also love to catch people on the social move, rumbled, red-handed, reading a bluffer's guide to polo. This mystifies Americans in particular, who are proud about getting richer, and will not only show you the bluffer's guide, but also the brand new polo shirts and the Buckaroo Ten-Speed Pony Simulator.

The British free trade in cracks about ugly women is legendary. The world admits to the fearsome power of women in many different ways – worshipping them, mutilating them, keeping them out of sight. The British technique is to make repulsive scolds of all females over the age of 37. 'Take my wife. *Please* take my wife . . .' If she's married, she's Mrs Andy Capp. If she's single, no one's surprised. She's Matron, or Madam Whiplash, she's the fat old broad on the postcards at Ramsgate, and recently she's been Mrs Thatcher. British men are not unique in their fear and loathing of proper women, but

in getting handsomely paid to display it on prime-time television they are notable, and so are the women who laugh with
them. Mediterranean women get politely cuckolded, Arab
women get proprietorially confined. Only British women get
re-drawn with three whiskery chins and parodied every pantomime season by men in frocks who are guaranteed to get all
the best laughs.

Outside of pantomime the British have no great taste for
slapstick. The inalienable right to titter has been theirs for so
long that they need something more sophisticated than a man
in a red nose. That's why they've become masters of bathos.
Virtuosi of the light, ironic touch. And the most inventive of
satirists in a land that has no sacred cows. The grown-up British
sense of humour is very grown-up indeed.

Other nations may buy it and dub it and watch it avidly, but
they don't always get it. Some, like the Japanese, are really still
in the Custard Pie phase of Humorous Evolution. They've still
got Silly Walks, Daft Voices, and Gentle Iconoclasm to work
through. They were late starters. And the British, in this at
least, have always headed the international field.

JAPAN

Very Far East Indeed

A city street. Men in grey suits are hurrying to another day of corporate high jinks. They have risen early, travelled in on a crowded train, and are prepared for a long session of shuffling paper and contemplating the company navel. They have left behind them wives they don't talk to, who keep the houses they can't really afford in immaculate good order and spend the rest of their time on serious shopping. And their children – who were once the angelic focus of their proudest hopes and dreams – their children are a constant worry because they don't want to shape up and wear a grey suit, and some of them are on the brink of doing something wild and shameful, like crossing against the lights. He could be Banstead Man, on his way to a life sentence in Lombard Street. But he isn't. This is Tokyo.

For all that we have in common with the Japanese, we two island nations, both of a sober and temperate tendency, we are foreign to one another. It is a very noticeable kind of foreignness. Though there are plenty of Brits living and working in Japan, there is no impression of a British presence on the city streets. Too few of us. And unlike the Japanese abroad, we don't go everywhere in multiples of ten. Every guided tour I

145

ever took in Japan was full of Iranians, Filipinos, and Hong Kong Chinese . . . and then us. We looked foreign. I'm small, with dark hair and pale skin. In Japan I look big and pink. My husband, who is big and pink, drew astonished stares.

But what do the Japanese think of us, we Giant Pink British Devils? They quite like us, that's what. In spite of the fact that we are loud, dirty, hasty, and cruel to our children, and in spite of the fact that we are the very worst thing of all – Not Japanese – they like us. Because we have an antique pedigree that we carry with impressive nonchalance. And we have a peerless mastery of wackiness. Non-stop street theatre in a Burton suit. A nation, in short, of 22-carat eccentrics.

Here are some of the things we do. Wear red ties. Roar with laugher. Jay walk. Take an hour for lunch. Prattle, stroll, whistle. Heckle and boo. Get up from our desk at 5.30 and say 'Stuff it!' See how easy it is to be an international wild child?

Many British businessmen arrive in Japan fully primed on the crowdedness, the costliness, and the mind-boggling industriousness of the place. They know that a cab from Narita airport into town is going to cost them 70 quid. They are certain it'll be raw fish all the way until they're safely back in Gateshead. And some of them, in the interests of doing a fast deal and not feeling an illiterate prat, have bought a Japanese phrase book. They are not well prepared.

I seriously question the value of toying with the Japanese language. Attempting to learn it is quite unlike learning another European language, because its function is not the same. The point about English or French or German is to convey ideas directly. Japanese pads hesitantly around the approximate environs of an idea. *Yes* and *No* are both situated somewhere deep within this linguistic quagmire. *Hai* may mean, 'Yes, I hear what you say and concur', or it may mean, 'Yes, I hear what you say and disagree/haven't decided/don't want to think about it yet'. *Iie* is the nearest the Japanese tongue gets to *No*. Not very near at all. Looking down into this conceptual abyss, smiling and bowing doesn't seem such a dumb option after all. Either you learn Japanese thoroughly, in which case you won't get much change out of ten years, or you abandon it and thank your lucky stars that English is still the language of the international market-place.

Having the language is one thing. Having the technique is another. British businessmen trained on the 3rd edition of Hal Heistwinkler's *Make That Sucker Sign!* find that they and all other Heistwinkler alumni get nowhere much in Japan.

In Japan the introductory formalities are slow and important. Consultations are thorough, attention to detail is tireless, and the favourite punctuation mark is the pregnant pause. Decisions, when they are eventually made, are submitted through the correct channels. In Japan everything is submitted through the correct channels. That's why we biddable, queue-forming Brits are able to appear racy and devil-may-care when we're standing next to the Japanese.

It is impossible to overstate the importance the Japanese attach to being able to *place* a person. Having a very highly developed sense of their own place – at Takafumi Piston Rings, in Japan Inc., and in the Universe – they like to know where you slot in. And so begins the business card business.

The casual British habit of taking someone's card and sticking it straight in a pocket is rude. It has the same effect as walking away from someone just as they are being introduced to you. In Japan your card *is* you. The giving and receiving must therefore be done with care and gravity.

You may think the main thing about a card is to have your

name on it, large and clear. Not so. That information is of minor importance. What matters is the name of your company, and especially your position in it. The Japanese, remember, want to be able to place you. If, like me, you are a self-employed loiterer and have nothing to put on a card except your name, you can save yourself the bother. It will be of little interest and no value.

When you receive a card – with a small, respectful bow that will be second nature to you after 48 hours in Japan – you should scrutinise it closely and make interested, scrutinising noises. After several minutes of this you have a choice. The preferred course is to place the card before you on the table and keep it there. The alternative, if pressure of time forces you to stow it away, is to put it carefully in a smart-looking card wallet. Never roll it, chew it, or use it to stop your chair from wobbling.

Compared with a typical Japanese company man, his British counterpart is a part-timer. He is also opinionated, contentious, and fickle. You may feel you are little more than a cog in the wheels of Cattermole Impact Adhesives, but by Japanese standards you are a free spirit. Sometimes you even put your feet up on your desk. It is important to know that Japanese men spend a lot of time in their offices. More time than you do,

148

and more time than they need to. It's interesting to know what they do there, and why.

What they do there is keep reminding themselves of their loyalties. They attend morning gatherings and listen attentively to the day's battle plans. In some companies they recite a kind of Corporate Creed for added inspiration. This is intended to rally men round the company flag and fetter the office grumbler. In Britain he rolls in at 9.35, reads the *Daily Mail* in the lavatory till the coffee trolley passes by, and spends the rest of the morning threatening to resign. If a British company circulated a corporate pep poem to be recited at a daily assembly, within the hour someone would have parodied it, photocopied it, and got a copy onto every desk in the building.

Once he's at his desk, the Japanese company man is reluctant to leave it. He could achieve what he needs to achieve in a much shorter working day, but why hurry away from the place where he knows he is cherished? His home is often an overcrowded nest. Living space is very tight, and children travel through the first four years of their life as Club Class cuckoos. By the time they have been indulged there isn't a lot of energy left for cherishing Father. But The Company is like Mother. A safe anchorage. And always dreaming up new ways of delighting him.

There are company trips, company dinners, company Sports Days. There are company baseball clubs, company Cherry Blossom outings, and company dormitories. All of these things help to bond a man to his company. Who could think of resigning with the next Company Recreation Day just around the corner? And anyway, what would the neighbours think of a man whose Company didn't want him there till eight o'clock at night?

As for upping sticks and going for a complete career change – that would be ungrateful behaviour indeed. Tell the Japanese that you started in Rubber Extrusions 18 years ago, moved on to Polyurethane Castings after five years, and then made the move from Bolton to Sudbury because of an irresistible offer in Sheetings, Ductings, and Mouldings, and they will think you are completely round the bend.

This kind of headstrong individualism does not necessarily disadvantage the British when they are in Japan. In small, and carefully timed doses it can make you seem captivatingly interesting. But it is also easy to take advantage of their overwhelming courtesy and go too far. Knowing how far is too far is much more important than knowing the Japanese for 'Can I have these trousers pressed for seven tomorrow morning.'

Too Far

How *not* to behave in Japan

1 Never eat in the street. Ronald McDonald has arrived in Japan but you should consume your Teriyaki Burger on the premises. Slurping noodles at a street corner noodle stall doesn't count as eating in the street.

2 Never blow your nose in public. I don't know why.

3 Never wear socks with holes. Some time during the day you will be obliged to take off your shoes.

4 Never ask your Japanese host to fix you up with a *geisha*

for the night. It's like him asking you to have Julia McKenzie sent up to his room.

5 Never indulge in back-slapping, hand-mangling, Call-Me-Tony-style buddying up.

Just far enough

How to be welcome in Japan

1 Shaking hands is not an unknown practice but it is an uncommon one. Bowing is easy and much more acceptable. Extravagantly deep bows should be avoided by Westerners, the loosely corseted, and anyone with back trouble.

2 Talking about the weather, showing people pictures of your kids, and remaining silent but smiling are all fine. Complaining, hectoring, and jabbing at the air with your finger are not.

3 Evening drinking sessions are expensive, exclusively male, and common business practice. Anyone liable to get invited should understand that the invitation is not optional. They should also practise sipping slowly, and know the words of at least one popular Western song. Being able to step up to the microphone in a *karaoke* bar and croon *Lady in Red* may bring you a step closer to brotherly understanding. The British and the Japanese are sadly united anyway in their use of alcohol to escape.

4 Think of a gift. Think of it not so much as a free will

offering, more as the opening salvo in a lavish war of attrition. Buy it, have it exquisitely wrapped, deliver it, and then wait for a superior, retaliatory parcel to be lobbed your way. That is merely foreplay. That has merely set the opening stakes so that escalation may begin.

I open with a bottle of Chivas Regal. You counter with two bottles of Taittinger Blanc de Blancs. Pleasantly stunned, I have matching His and Hers Polo Shirts sent round from Ralph Lauren, but before I know it you are on the doorstep with a Lucky Bag from Hermes. Down, but still not out, I make a call to my nearest Cartier dealer . . . Get the picture? It contrasts sharply with accepted British practice of exchanging company diaries round about March 15th. In Japan whole floors of department stores are dedicated to the display of Gift Suggestions. Boxes of tea, boxes of soap, cases of liquor, parcels of beef, trays of perfect polished apples. In Japan, when in doubt about giving, definitely give.

The polite Japanese response to a proferred gift is '*Iie*', which as you will remember from Lesson One, kind of means 'No', and in this instance kind of means, 'You shouldn't have, but thanks anyway.'

5 Be prepared to play golf. Be prepared to get up in the middle of the night to play it, and to feel deeply honoured, because in Japan people wait years to get a game. It is essential to be punctual. That means not late but not early either. And because you're anxious not to be late you will inevitably be early and must hide until your host has arrived. Your schedule for a day's golf will therefore run something like this: 11 pm, midnight, and 1 am – Wake in a nervous sweat convinced you've

152

overslept. 2.30 am – Drive to the golf course in odd socks because you did oversleep. 3.15 am – Arrive at golf course and hide. 4.30 am – Tee Off. 9 am – Lunch. 10.30 am – Resume at the 10th Hole.

Do not talk shop.

And does the Japanese first impression of us hold up? Are we loud, hasty, and dirty? Yes. We soap ourselves in the bath and then lie slopping around in the scum. We train our voices for the well-projected baritone effect, especially us girls who want to get anywhere in life. And we seriously believe we can do business on the strength of a Hal Heistwinkler handshake, shoddily prepared meetings, and a few drinks with the chaps. A flair for wing-and-a-prayer methods is something we quietly admire in colleagues. Small talk is irksome, detail is tedious, and we just want a signature on that contract and a seat on the next flight home.

British companies who sincerely want to do business with the Japanese are now learning not to send Flash Harry to Japan. In his place they are sending a slower moving animal. A self-effacing man of modest habits. Someone who has done his homework, practised with chopsticks, and packed his bag with plenty of brand new socks. They are telling him not to hurry back. They are telling him to smile and warble soothingly. Not to worry if he doesn't get the deal first time out because Japan is only the other side of the world and he can easily pop back for further exploratory discussions.

They are sending a man with a very big business card indeed.

Ten Tips for Business Travellers to Japan

1 Never make cold calls in Japan.

2 Work out how long it's going to take to get to your destination. Then double it.

3 Japanese taxis overturn everything you've ever learned at the mercy of a London cabbie. They show a red light when they're for hire, and a green light when they're taken. Tipping doesn't exist. It's difficult to persuade a driver to take you a short distance. And the concept of fleecing the foreigner is quite unknown. The problem for foreigners in Japan is persuading a taxi to pick them up at all. Look at it this way. A Japanese cabbie's dream fare is pre-booked, paid for by a company, and will take him on a two-hour trip to the suburbs, to a destination someone can direct him to with confidence. Besides, the trains are terrific.

4 When using the trains it is not enough to know the name of the station. It's essential to know which subway exit to use. Some Tokyo stations are small underground cities. Taking the wrong exit can leave you miles off course with an important meeting missed.

5 The Japanese are slow to use first names. A surname suffixed with -*san* is the correct form. However, to award yourself the honour of -*san*, as in Ormethwaite-san, is strictly not done.

6 Go well supplied with high quality business cards, immaculate socks, and time.

7 Leave your wife (or your husband) home in Nuneaton. The Japanese will not invite you back to their place because they worry it may not be grand enough and anyway it would take all evening to get there. Socialising is confined to the public arena – restaurants and theatre for foreign businesswomen, bars, bars, and more bars for businessmen.

8 Business drinking can be hectic and may give rise to this dilemma: do I keep knocking it back and suffer tomorrow, or do I risk snubbing that all-important group spirit by staying more sober than everyone else? Pitching your behaviour to cast a flattering light on others is a basic precept of Japanese life.

9 Never bad-mouth anyone or anything with which you are associated. The Japanese don't do business with people who lack loyalty.

10 Slow down. The Japanese are meticulous and thorough, and they only strike deals when they're happy about everything, especially their prospective business partners. The up-side of all this caution and deliberation is that they nearly always get things right, and they hardly ever sue. Time is the best possible investment you can make in Japan. And as I discovered at the end of my travels, it's a long way to go back if you forget something.

BACK HOME

I began this book in a spirit of black humour. I already had a lot of ideas about the British abroad. As usual I was not travelling with an open mind. I prepared to set off with the grim mission of confirming the worst.

Immediately my life began to fill with unaccommodating people who would not fit my stereotypes. Brits who had been intrepid, independent travellers, Brits who were accomplished linguists. They surfaced at every party and dinner and whittled away at the very idea that the British are an international joke and there might be a book in it.

Then I started travelling, beginning as so many Brits do, with a daytrip to France. My fellow passengers weren't bad. Just loud, rude, and full to the eyeballs with gung-ho ignorance and alcohol. Still I and they were treated with a kind forbearance that was to recur everywhere I went in the world. And anyway, I had worse to experience than Boulogne. I had yet to go to tourist Spain.

As holidaymakers we only seek the same thing as every other nation that can afford holidays – *otherness*. Something more piquant than staying home but not too much of it. We don't exactly want to go to Spain which is, after all, a harsh, uncompromising jigsaw of people and terrain. What we want is a British hotel experience, inclusive of soft toilet paper and gravy on our dinners, and a few, brief, tamed Spanish interludes. Flamenco Show Nite every Wednesday at 8.

The door to wrinkle-free holidays now stands wide open, but another door is closing. We are less and less qualified to go and stare at the world's picturesquely destitute. We're becoming them. Eventually in Salou, the Spanish will photograph the barefoot, illiterate Brits.

Wherever I went, my original stereotypes appeared on cue. Apparently it was the closed season for culturally-informed tourism and business travel and the question uppermost in every British mind, from Benidorm to Abu Dhabi, was, 'Where can we get a proper cup of tea?' I never heard anyone call 'British Go Home'. I wondered why.

The sound of British voices began to make my heart sink. I knew they would be asking for recent news on the weather in Essex, or the whereabouts of a shop that stocked Weetabix. But I had a job to do. I followed them to the ends of the earth. Each journey I made deepened one of my first impressions of the British abroad – that the prevalence of our language has fed the illusion that we occupy the global centre stage, but that in truth our position is marginal. That we often behave badly abroad is admitted, but not dwelt on. Like the parents of a disagreeable child, Europe seems to have decided to deprive us of the oxygen of attention. Either we must learn to be civil or be sent to our island.

The harshness of that message was diluted outside of Europe, but it was still there. In Arabia and in America I found a strong sense of old affections and credits that were still good, but running out. There is a limit to the charm of eccentricity, and the British have pushed theirs as far as it will go.

We hardly change. And yet change used to be something we excelled at. Everywhere around us nations are growing up, or growing older and wiser. People we could once show a thing or two could now show us, except that they're too polite. We have airs and graces that belie our reduced circumstances, and we still don't see the point of learning French.

This is no insurmountable task I'm proposing. It is actually within the grasp of the British to be better exports than they are at present. All it would take would be a little self-examination, an honest look at where we stand in the world, and some imagination. It isn't that the British are congenitally stupid or obnoxious. More that they enjoy seeing themselves as normal and everyone else as flawed rejects.

Travel could be the saving of us, as long as the countries we visit resist our idea that the British way is best. If our hosts get tougher with us we shall learn fast. And if they stop bailing us out with tea bags and perfect English we shall be able to overcome our fear of something new.

My journeys were populated with all the stereotypes I had planned to meet – sweaty executives, drunks in Union Jack vests, women with suitcases full of Digestive biscuits. But none of them excited the mirth or loathing I'd predicted. The world, it seemed, had better things to do than notice the British.

I also met a very few Brits whose traveller's curiosity was greater than their fear of diarrhoea. Travellers of the old school who expect discomfort and danger as well as exhilaration. The kind of travellers Britain used to be so good at producing because we were all raised to be Spartans. They were rewarded by astonished delight from the natives, and so, occasionally, was I. In Italy when I tried to roll my Rs and twirl my linguine onto my fork, I was complimented on being French. In Spain, I walked like a lady and they hazarded I might be Italian. I allowed this to go to my head only briefly. In New York they took one look at my stunted shoulder pads and knew exactly where I was from.

INDEX